This book was made possible through the generous assistance of:

Kodak Eastman Kodak Company

PAN AM

Nikon

AVIS

HB BETTOJA HOTELS

Credito Italiano

Sarah Leen

First published 1990 by Collins Publishers San Francisco
A Division of HarperCollins Publishers

Project Directors: Jennifer Erwitt and Roy Rowan
Design Director: Jennifer Barry

Title page photograph by: Michael Yamashita

Library of Congress Cataloging-in-Publication Data
A day in the life of Italy: photographed by 100 of the world's
leading photojournalists on one day, April 27, 1990.
    p. cm.
    ISBN 0-00-215729-2
    1. Italy—Description and travel—1975- —Views.
2. Italy—Social life and customs—Pictorial works.
I. Collins Publishers San Francisco.
DG420.D35 1990
945'.0022'2—dc20   90-38792

Printed and bound in Japan
First printing August 1990

10 9 8 7 6 5 4 3 2 1

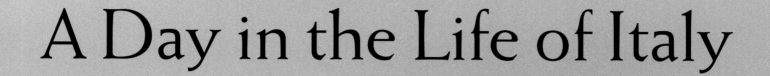

A Day in the Life of Italy

Photographed by 100 of the
world's leading photojournalists
on one day, April 27, 1990

This book is dedicated to Ethan Hoffman

Collins Publishers San Francisco
A Division of HarperCollinsPublishers

Porto San Giorgio, 5:45 AM: "He who sleeps," goes the Italian
proverb, "catches no fish."
Photographer: Patrick Tehan, USA

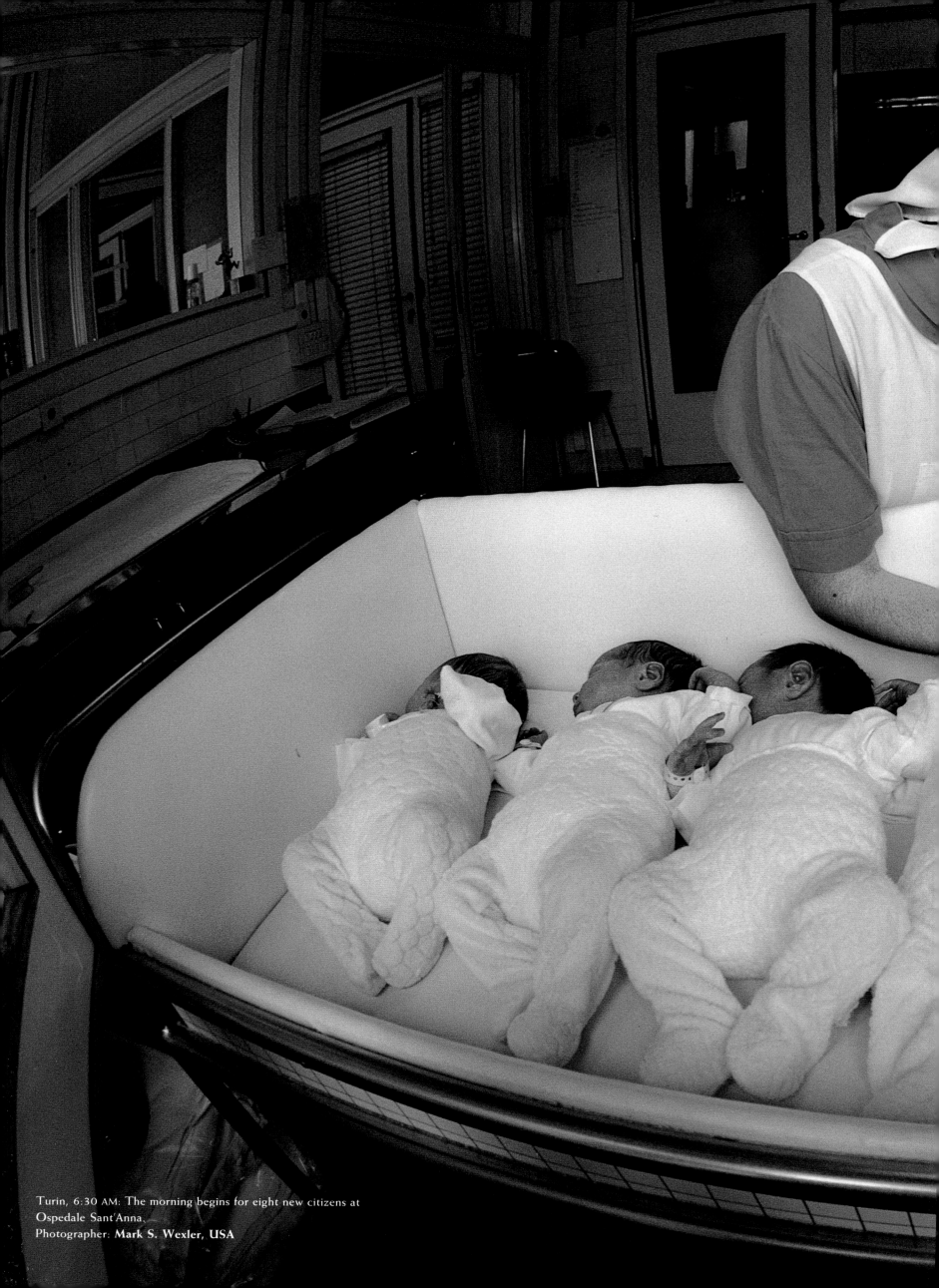

Turin, 6:30 AM: The morning begins for eight new citizens at
Ospedale Sant'Anna.
Photographer: **Mark S. Wexler, USA**

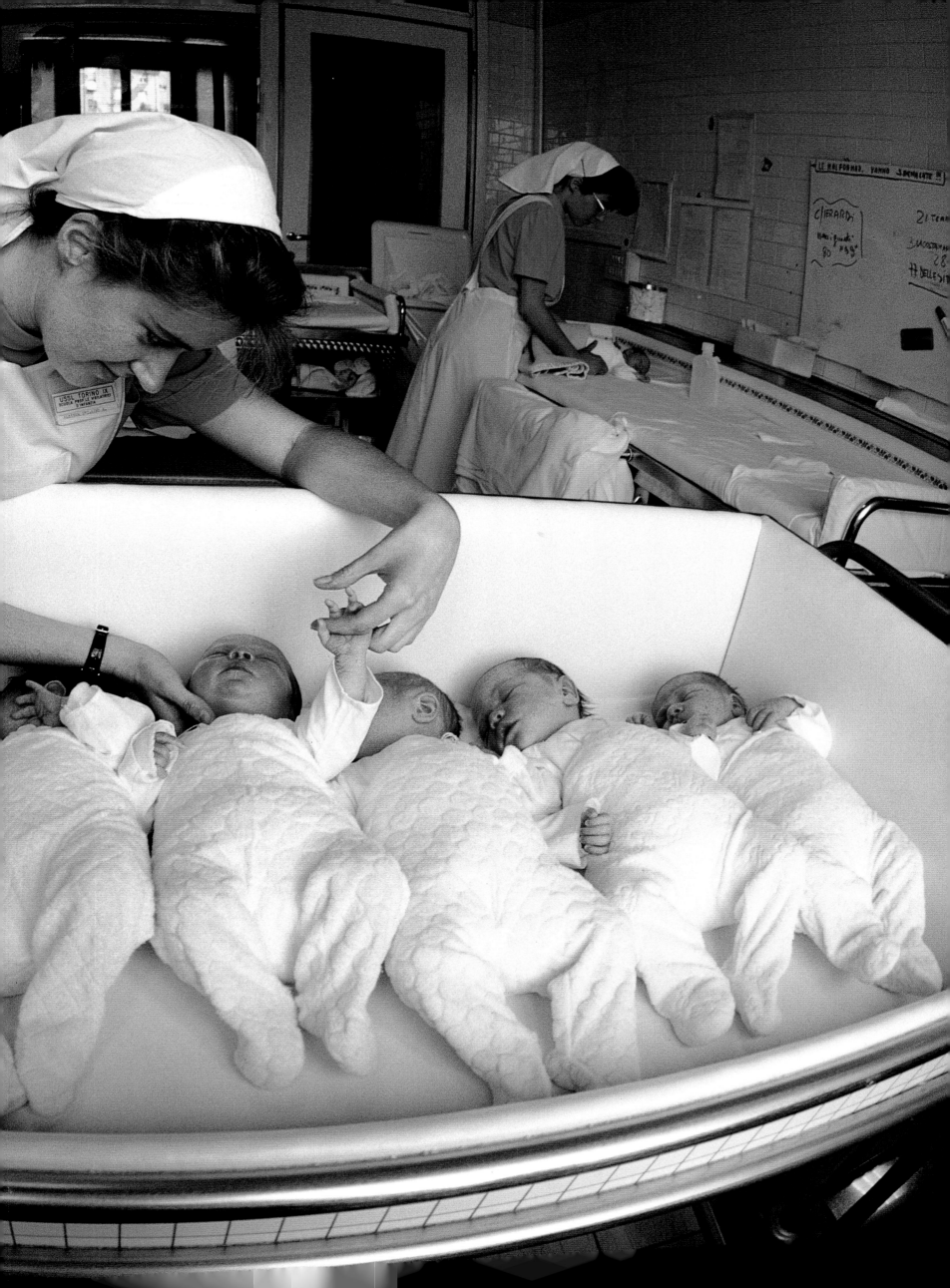

Vercelli, 7:00 AM: Farm workers spray flooded paddies in the rice-growing capital of Europe.
Photographer: **Marcello Bertinetti, Italy**

Venice, 7:30 AM: The eastern sun comes to the island city, for
centuries a formidable maritime republic.
Photographer: **Claus C. Meyer, Germany**

Italy is proof that life is not fair. It's a small country, really, a slender peninsula jutting into the Mediterranean with two major islands. Yet it has the great majority of the West's art and architectural treasures, a sensual climate that has inspired dreamers and lovers for thousands of years, one of the world's great cuisines, and mountains, valleys, beaches, and cities that bleed with color and sparkle with light. What trick is this, played on the rest of the world? What's left for the rest of us?

It's a trick that delights, ultimately, because Italy's very excessiveness is its charm. Why have one language when you can have dozens of dialects? Why have one world-class city when you can have several? And why travel around the globe for a lifetime when you can see nearly as much in Italy in a year—or even, in the case of April 27, 1990, a day?

What the photographers who blanketed Italy on that day found was more than a land blessed many times over. They found a country standing on, and in many cases breaking away from, a past filled with Roman caesars and Renaissance painters. The epochs hurtle against one another as Italy approaches the 1992 unification of Europe, and the results are often surprising.

The agricultural economy has given way to the industrial, and Italy has quietly become one of the world's richest nations, with an annual gross domestic product of $825 billion. Typically for a people who have always distrusted centralization and large-scale enterprises, the burst into the world's economic elite has been fueled not by mega-corporations, but by thousands of mid-sized companies and family-owned businesses. With wealth has come new urgency to an old problem, however, for the lire washing through the streets of Milan and Turin have served to underscore the traditional gulf between the country's monied north and its threadbare south.

The role of the Catholic Church, too, is changing. While its treasures dominate many a small town and draw millions of tourists to Rome each year, it is no longer the official state religion, and the Pope can no longer insist that city authorities in Rome ban films, plays, or books that the Holy See finds objectionable. Both divorce and abortion are now legal.

Fortunately, change has its limits. There are no plans to raze the Pantheon, and much of the country looks as it has for years, decades, and in some cases centuries—albeit several shades dirtier for the wear of modern pollution. The respect for history in Italy is all the more impressive because impulse and freneticism are everywhere, as ubiquitous as the cappuccino at dawn and the yellow light of sunset.

Give yourself over to this excessive land of impulse and history, maddening as it may be; the country overwhelms those who resist. And as you turn the pages of this moment in Italian history, may you find yourself as smitten as the poet Robert Browning, who wrote more than a century ago:

Open my heart, and you will see
Graved inside of it, 'Italy'.

—Bernard Ohanian

A Day in the Life of
ITALY

February 14, 1990

Dear Photographer:

It's a great pleasure to invite you to participate in the tenth shoot in the *Day in the Life* series, *A Day in the Life of Italy*. On April 27, you and 99 other top photojournalists from around the world will share a unique challenge: to record in a single 24-hour period the vitality, diversity, and passion of an ancient culture in the midst of profound change.

In Italy, the mark of history is everywhere – in the Roman ruins that dot the landscape, in Renaissance frescoes illuminating forgotten chapels, in faces that recall Caesar and Brutus. But there's far more than history to this vibrant land. Italy has quietly grown into one of the world's great economic success stories, without sacrificing the lust for food, art, and the good life for which it is justifiably renowned.

The project has several goals: first and foremost, to create a memorable visual document that answers a few questions about Italy and perhaps asks a few more; to involve the people of Italy in a celebration of photography; and finally, to bring together people of talent and provide them with an opportunity to work together.

Although you will receive a specific assignment, you're free to photograph whatever you find on shoot day. Remember, though, that we're not setting out to make the definitive statement about Italy. Nor will we concentrate on the rich, the famous, or the powerful. Instead, we ask that you apply your skills to one of the toughest jobs in photojournalism: to make extraordinary pictures of ordinary, everyday events.

Following the shoot, your work will be reviewed by a distinguished group of picture editors:

Guy Cooper, *Newsweek*
Mike Davis, *Albuquerque Tribune*
Sandra Eisert, *San Jose Mercury News*
Alfonso Gutiérrez Escera, *A.G.E. Fotostock*
Peter Howe, *Life*

Michele McNally, *Fortune*
Maddy Miller, *People*
Amilcare Ponchielli, *Corriere della Sera*
Michele Stephenson, *Time*
Susan Vermazen, *New York*

Richard Eskite

The best photographs will be incorporated in a large-format hardcover book and a traveling exhibit of photographic prints. The sponsors of *A Day in the Life of Italy* – Eastman Kodak, Pan Am, Nikon, Bettoja Hotels, Avis, and Credito Italiano – understand the journalistic nature of the project and have agreed, without exception, to forgo any editorial control. *A Day in the Life of Italy* will be an honest look at Italy, not just another book of pretty picture postcards.

Of course, there is no guarantee that every photographer will get a picture in the book. Whether or not your work is published depends not only on your hard work and creativity, but also on what kind of luck (and weather) you have on Friday, April 27.

The schedule: On Sunday, April 22, photojournalists from 14 countries will fly into Rome on Pan Am. At Monday's initial briefing you will receive 50 rolls of Kodak film and information about your assignment. Kodak's photography workshop for Italian schoolchildren and a group portrait at Rome's Campidoglio will follow. On Tuesday you will meet with your editor to go over the details of your assignment, and on Wednesday you will travel to your shooting location (we will provide you with a rental car courtesy of Avis if your assignment requires it). Thursday is left open for you to explore your location. Friday's shoot begins at midnight, and on Saturday you will return to Rome before heading home.

Each *Day in the Life* project has posed a unique set of challenges, and *A Day in the Life of Italy* will be no exception. You'll need all the patience, insight, and imagination you can muster, but there's never been a better place to get great pictures. With enough people of your caliber and experience working on it, the project is destined to be a great success.

At this writing, 30 of us at Collins are putting all the pieces in place to make sure your shoot goes smoothly. If working with us in Italy appeals to you, please read the enclosed forms and agreement carefully and return them to us no later than February 28. See you in Rome.

Best regards,

Jennifer Erwitt
Project Directors

Roy Rowan

Monica Almeida

● *Previous page*

Buon giorno, Mamma: Two-year-old Sergio Donati greets the day with his mother Stefania.
Photographer:
Monica Almeida, USA

● *Left*

On the job since 2:30 AM, baker Giuseppe Mammi knocks back an espresso in the town of Recco. Mammi's love for *il caffè* is shared by his friends and countrymen: The average Italian consumes 9.5 pounds of coffee a year. Per capita, only the West Germans, French, and Americans drink more.
Photographer:
Michael Bryant, USA

● *Above*

Cappuccino, cartoons, and a day-old *International Herald Tribune* help American fashion model Hunter Reno shake the sleep from her eyes at her studio apartment in Milan.
Photographer:
Dana Fineman, USA

● *Above*

In a daily ritual, Romans clog the ancient streets with their modern-day chariots as they inch toward work and school. Smog from the cars of Rome's three million residents is no mere nuisance: Traffic cops are occasionally overcome by the fumes, and many of the city's ancient monuments are crumbling to dust, victims of auto exhaust and damaging vibrations from passing vehicles. Like many Italian cities, Rome has closed much of its central district to cars—protecting some monuments, but placing an additional burden on the streets that remain open.

Photographer:
Edoardo Fornaciari, Italy

● *Right*

The streets of Maremma: Francesco Basville, a John Wayne fan who is one of Italy's last remaining *butteri*, or cowboys, wrangles cattle at the Maremma Regional Natural Park in Tuscany. Some 450 cows and 100 horses live in the park's animal reserve—the only one of its kind in Italy—along with wild boar, foxes, and other animals. The southwestern part of Tuscany was once covered with large ranches, most of which have now been divided into smaller farms. Today up to 500 people might show up on a typical day to watch Basville and his fellow 'pokes practice a dying art.

Photographer:
Jay Dickman, USA

● *Left*

Me and my shadow: Mafia buster Giuseppe Ajala, Italy's most famous prosecutor, arrives at his office in Palermo accompanied by his ever-present bodyguard. Ajala, who was the lead prosecutor in a landmark trial that resulted in the imprisonment of more than 400 underworld figures in 1986, always travels in an armored car, and at times is surrounded by as many as 30 armed escorts. The fears for Ajala's safety are well-founded: Dozens of prosecutors, judges, and journalists were murdered in the late 1980s after crusading against the Sicilian Mafia and Italy's two other large underworld organizations, the Naples-based *Camorra* and the Calabria-based *'ndrangheta*. The three organizations have used construction scams, sophisticated money-laundering schemes, the international drug trade, and old-fashioned shakedowns to create a combined annual income of about $75 billion—making them, in the estimation of a leading Italian research agency, "our biggest private industry."

Photographer:

David C. Turnley, USA

● *Above*

A nose for news: Passers-by pause at a newsstand in Reggio di Calabria. More than 100 daily newspapers are published in Italy, including four national sports dailies and papers published by each of the major political parties. The big three among national general-interest dailies are *La Stampa*, *Corriere della Sera*, and *la Repubblica*. Other top sellers include Milan's *Gazzetta dello Sport* as well as *l'Unità*, the Communist Party daily.

Photographer:

Raphaël Gaillarde, France

Jean-Pierre Laffont

● *Previous page*

Prop duster: Danilo DiBagno does some housekeeping at Rome's famed Cinecittà studio, where filmmakers like Federico Fellini, Bernardo Bertolucci, Vittorio De Sica, Lina Wertmüller, Francis Coppola, and Roberto Rossellini have worked their cinematic magic.
Photographer:
Jean-Pierre Laffont, France

● *Above*

Tying one on: Marco Crocchianti, Juri Conti, Marco Rubini, and Luca Porchetti get dressed for another day of school at the Istituto Professionale Alberghiero in Spoleto. Teenagers come from throughout Europe to enroll at the Istituto, which offers high school diplomas with specializations in cooking, hotel administration, and waiting and bartending.
Photographer:
Bill Greene, USA

● *Right*

Who's the fairest of them all: Fashion models (*left to right*) Hunter Reno, 22, Helena Jesus, 24, Katalin Anita Kovács, 21, and Missy Hargraves, 22, primp for portfolio shots at the studios of Riccardo Gay Model Management in Milan. These and other young women from around the world come to Italy's second-largest city with dreams of joining the more than one thousand models who live and work in what has become one of the world's leading centers of high fashion.
Photographer:
Dana Fineman, USA

● *Above*

Serving those who sit and wait, a 15-year-old student at the Istituto Professionale Alberghiero practices his chosen trade on a pair of fellow would-be *camerieri*. Tourism's role as Italy's leading industry makes waiting on tables a serious business.
Photographer:
Bill Greene, USA

● *Right*

Gerardo di Pirro, a 20-year veteran of the *carabinieri*, or Italian military police, steals a moment with his four-year-old daughter Marianna while on break from his duties in the mountain town of Ovindoli. While officially an arm of the military, the carabinieri carry out normal police duties alongside the national and local police forces. Di Pirro says he's never been fired upon, *"grazie a Dio,"* even in the days of widespread political violence in the 1970s and early 1980s.
Photographer:
Monica Almeida, USA

● *Left*

Her workbook open to a translation of Carl Sandburg's famous poem *Fog*, a uniformed elementary school girl in the town of Asolo expresses herself with her hands and face where words won't do. Italian children are required to attend school only until age 14, one of the lowest such ages among Western industrialized countries. In elementary school, however, students and teachers in Italy benefit from one of the best ratios in the world—one teacher for every thirteen pupils.
Photographer:
Annie Griffiths Belt, USA

● *Above*

A pair of kindergarten buddies share a smile at the Scuola Materna Statale in Ovindoli. Like kindergartners everywhere, according to teacher Cecilia DiMichele, these *bambini* favor coloring, finger painting, building with blocks, and working with clay.
Photographer:
Monica Almeida, USA

● *Above*

Like everything else in Venice, the fruits and vegetables travel by boat. But the romance is fading from this magical city: Untreated waste has flowed into the waterways for centuries, leaving three feet of sludge at the bottom of the canals. Only the tides, the highest of which annually force residents and visitors alike to walk on wooden planks a foot or two above the ground, keep the muck from totally overwhelming the city. Smog from nearby industrial refineries is eating away at art treasures as well. With the population of Venice's islands having dropped by half since the end of World War II, civic leaders are wondering aloud whether their city has become a "lagoon Disneyland"–a city that exists solely for the pleasure of the 20 million people who visit the islands each year.

Photographer:
Ethan Hoffman, USA

● *Right*

Haggling over flat-leaf parsley, women in Bassano del Grappa get their day's shopping under way at an outdoor market in a downtown square. Despite the introduction of American-style supermarkets in recent years, tradition and the quest for freshness lead many Italians to continue to shop for food every morning, with visits to the bakery, the deli, the butcher, and the produce market.

Photographer:
Annie Griffiths Belt, USA

● Left and above

Farmers' market: Some 500 rice growers, brokers, and buyers meet every Tuesday and Friday morning at the Borsa del Riso in Vercelli, a provincial capital of 50,000, to haggle over the price of one of Italy's most important agricultural products. While Italy is known the world over for its pasta, its annual rice output of more than a million tons makes it Western Europe's leading producer. Almost all of the country's rice fields are found in the four northern regions of Piedmont, Lombardy, Veneto and Emilia-Romagna, where rice rivals pasta in popularity at many a dining room table.
Photographer:
Marcello Bertinetti, Italy

● *Left*

Paolina Di Michele, 77, tends to her chickens outside her house in Ovindoli.
Photographer:
Monica Almeida, USA

● *Above*

A vendor at the fish market in Mazara del Vallo looks for a customer to snap up his merchandise. The Sicilian city is considered to be Italy's most important fishing port, with virtually all of its 50,000 people either directly or indirectly employed in the fish-ing industry. More than 10,000 Tunisians live here, supplying cheap and often illegal labor to the owners of fishing boats.
Photographer:
Ernesto Bazan, Italy

● *Above*

The sights are as varied as the fare in the ubiquitous Italian bar, where the menu usually includes coffee, alcohol, ice cream, snacks, and pastries. Customers often eat standing up at the counter; in many bars, table seating comes at a premium.
Photographer:
Dilip Mehta, Canada

● *Right*

La dolce vita gets an early start at an outdoor cafe in Rome's Piazza del Popolo. Spring officially begins in the capital when tourists and residents alike start taking their cappuccino, espresso, and ice cream outdoors at cafes in Piazza Navona, Piazza della Rotonda, and Piazza del Popolo.
Photographer:
Rudi Frey, Austria

● *Above*

This land is my land: Sicilian winemaker Carmelo Scandurra tastes a glass of *vino bianco* from his family vineyard in Santa Maria di Licodia, at the foot of Mt. Etna. "When I sleep, I dream about this land," says Scandurra of the tract where he was born 66 years ago. "It is better than money. It is the best thing in all the world."
Photographer:
Richard Marshall, USA

● *Right*

A castle in Torrechiara stands guard over the vineyards in Emilia-Romagna, one of Italy's leading wine-producing regions. No other country produces, consumes, or exports more wine than Italy, where vineyards cover fully 1 percent of the national territory. The average Italian drinks about 24 gallons of wine each year; enough is left from the 2 billion gallons produced annually to export about 25 million gallons to the United States, accounting for half the U.S. wine imports from Europe. Recognizing the importance of wine to the Italian economy, the government has designated more than 200 wine-producing areas as "premium." Wines produced in these areas carry on their labels the phrase *"Denominazione di origine controllata."*
Photographer:
Joe McNally, USA

● *Following page*

"The woods have sharp ears," according to a Latin proverb, making this grove in Castelfidardo the perfect place for Tullio Alessandrini to try out the sound of a new accordion. While in hiding after the German invasion of Italy in the latter stages of World War II, Alessandrini taught himself to play what Italians call *la fisarmonica;* he later became a professional tester for Soprani Antico, a Castelfidardo-based accordion manufacturer. Now in semi-retirement, he still tests the occasional accordion, leads tours of the local accordion museum, and plays at parties in restaurants—"for fun," he quickly points out, "not for money."
Photographer:
Steve Krongard, USA

Steve Krumbach

● *Above*

Maintenance call: A pair of nuns
pay their regular visit to see that
all is well at an empty convent
building in Serramazzoni, in the
hills south of Modena.
Photographer:
George Steinmetz, USA

● *Above*

A swift red flash, Ferrari's F40
gets a checkup at the company's
test track in Maranello, just outside the city of Modena. The
limited-production car, released
in 1990 to mark the fortieth
anniversary of the company
founded by the late Enzo Ferrari,
has about 3-1/2 times the horse-
power of a typical family sedan
and can go from zero to sixty in
3.5 seconds. It can empty the
wallet just as quickly, with some
European dealers getting close
to a million dollars for the car.
Photographer:
George Steinmetz, USA

Glass masters: Roberto Boscolo
shapes a fruit bowl while Luciano Zanchi blows the hot
glass at the firm of Cenedese e
Albarelli on the Venetian island
of Murano. The two men, who
are among 6,000 glass workers
on Murano, each come from
generations of glassblowers and
have spent years perfecting their
technique. In the method of
glassblowing traditionally used
in Venice, a block of glass is
heated to 2,000 degrees Fahrenheit; in the few minutes before
it cools, the glassblower blows
it into a bubble while a second
person spins it and shapes it using specially designed wooden
blocks. Boscolo is considered
the *maestro* at Cenedese e Albarelli, which was commis-
sioned to create special glasses
for the economic summit held
in Venice in 1987.
Photographer:
Claus C. Meyer, Germany

● *Left*

Doll house: In Naples, Luigi
Grassi examines a doll outside
the business founded by his
grandfather and namesake in
1899. At the Ospedale delle
Bambole, or doll hospital, Grassi, his wife Patrizia, and their
two daughters repair antique
dolls, crèche figurines, and por-
celain figures, charging as much
as $160 and as little as $25 for
their handiwork. The family's
own collection of antique dolls
numbers about a hundred.
Photographer:
Bruno Barbey, France

● *Above*

At home in the realm of gold,
Donatella Balestra exhibits some
of her designs at the Balestra
gold factory in Bassano del
Grappa. The dynamic Signora
Balestra is the chief stylist for the
company, which was founded in
1882 and produces jewelry for
merchants the world over.
Photographer:
John Dominis, USA

● *Right*

Making time: Craftsman Dario Lagomarsino shows off his handiwork at the Roberto Trebino clock factory in Uscio, a small town near Genoa. Lagomarsino and his 20 colleagues at the family-run business, which has been in operation since 1824, turn out about 400 completed timepieces a year, primarily for churches.
Photographer:
Michael Bryant, USA

● *Above*

The merchant of Florence: In the drawing room of the historic Palazzo Feroni, Leonardo Ferragamo, 31, chooses shoes for his family firm's new collection with assistants Patrizia Steccato, Ilaria Papucci, and Francesca Brunori. Leonardo's father, Salvatore, founded the world-famous Ferragamo line of shoes after moving to the United States in 1914, executing many of his first designs for top movie stars. Upon his return to Florence in 1926, Salvatore Ferragamo began expanding the company's repertoire, which now includes accessories and formal and casual wear for men and women alike. All six Ferragamo children work for the company, which has been headed by their mother Wanda since Salvatore's death in 1960.

Photographer:

Guglielmo de' Micheli, Italy

● *Above*

Silvana Masiero turns out another pattern at Ratti S.p.A.,
one of 400 fabric factories in
the provincial capital of Como,

● *Following page*

Designing man: Bearded
Gianfranco Ferré, one of Europe's leading fashion innova-
tors, works with model Stepha-

Volker Hinz

Romano Cagnoni

● *Previous page*

Carving art from stone, as craftsmen in Pietrasanta have done from sculptors' models for centuries, Sergio Buratti and Mauro Galeotti hammer out giant reproductions of Michelangelo's *David* and the ancient Greek masterwork *Venus de Milo*. Michelangelo himself made frequent trips to the nearby marble quarries, located on the Tuscan coast at the foot of the Apuane Alps. These statues were ordered by a Japanese importer, who plans to put them on public display in Osaka.
Photographer:
Romano Cagnoni, Italy

● *Above*

Visitors to the National Museum in Reggio di Calabria study two of the world's most famous Greeks, the statues known as the Riace Bronzes. The pair, sculpted in the fifth century B.C. during the 600-year period of Greek rule in Calabria, were fished from the Ionian Sea near the town of Riace in 1972.
Photographer:
Raphaël Gaillarde, France

● *Right*

Making a point: A monk leads a tour of the Abbey of Monte Oliveto Maggiore in the Tuscan hills. Italy's national art treasures, of which these frescoes depicting the life of St. Benedict are a part, are becoming an endangered species. Close to 50 works of art disappear every day, most of them falling into the hands of smugglers who whisk them out of the country. The smugglers have come to the right place; United Nations officials estimate that Italy is home to 80 percent of Europe's historically significant architecture and visual art.
Photographer:
Pedro Coll, Spain

● *Above*

For art's sake: In one of thousands of such projects currently under way in an effort to save Italy's irreplaceable artistic legacy, professional restorers Sabino Giovannoni and Maria Rosa Lanfranchi touch up a fresco 15 stories above the floor of Florence's famed Santa Maria del Fiore Church. The pair first treat the painting with chemicals to soak away dirt and soot, then repair and repaint sections where the plaster has cracked or fallen away. The fresco is one of several painted by Giorgio Vasari and Federico Zuccari between 1572 and 1578 to cover the inside of Santa Maria del Fiore's dome.

Photographer:
Guglielmo de' Micheli, Italy

● *Right*

Though ravaged by earthquakes, pillagers, and more than 1,900 years of exposure to the elements, the Colosseum endures, the eternal symbol of the Eternal City. Built on marshland and opened formally in A.D. 80 with 100 straight days of games and shows, the four-deck, 50,000-seat amphitheatre was scorned after the Christianization of the Roman Empire, with church leaders decrying its history of violence and hedonism. Renaissance architects later stripped *il Colosseo* of its marble in order to build Rome's Palazzo Barberini, Palazzo Venezia, and St. Peter's Basilica; the pillaging stopped only after Pope Benedict XIV declared the Colosseum sanctified in 1749. Although its floor has since been removed to show the underground passageways where performers and animals waited their turn before facing the throngs, the venerable oval still reaches 150 feet into the Roman sky, comforting those who believe the ancient proverb: "As long as the Colosseum stands, Rome shall stand; when the Colosseum falls, Rome shall fall; and when Rome falls, the world will end."

Photographer:
Paul Chesley, USA

● *Above*

Antonio Laurieri puts the finishing touches on *focaccia* bread in his family's bakery. Focaccia, which is distinguished from pizza by its lack of cheese, is but one of several kinds of bread turned out daily by the Panificio Lucano in the city of Matera. Baking remains a noble profession in a country where the English-language expression "as good as gold" comes out as "as good as bread," and where instead of giving you "the shirt off his back" a generous soul offers "the bread from his mouth."
Photographer:
Gerd Ludwig, Germany

● *Right*

Close-knit friends Pasqua Fusco, Agata Spacone, and Maria Filla spend the morning talking on the steps of a house in their hometown of Scanno, in the Abruzzo region. Fusco and Filla are widows and wear black every day in a tradition slowly disappearing in modern Italy.
Photographer:
Stephanie Maze, USA

● *Above*

Reel life: Owner of a newly minted Oscar, 34-year-old director Giuseppe Tornatore, the latest boy wonder of the Italian cinema, checks a take at his Rome studio. Tornatore's *Cinema Paradiso* was named best foreign language film by the Academy of Motion Picture Arts and Sciences on March 26, 1990. His next project, *Stanno Tutti Bene*, stars film legend Marcello Mastroianni.

Photographer:
Steve McCurry, USA

● *Right*

Garstone Nardo inspects a gondola in need of repair, while his son Ettore touches up another boat in the background. The pair's shop, Lo Squero, has been building the elegant boats for nearly 300 years, and is one of only two gondola shops left in Venice. Today their primary business is gondola repair and restoration, but they still turn out five new gondolas a year. "A well-made gondola," says Ettore with pride, "usually lasts about 25 years."

Photographer:
Ethan Hoffman, USA

● *Left and above*

Island in the sun: About 5,000
people live on Burano, about 45
minutes from Venice on a slow
boat. The island, located in the
north part of the Venetian lagoon, is still a working fishing
port and is renowned for its
hand-stitched embroidered lace.
Photographer:
Georg Gerster, Switzerland

● *Left*

Venice boatman: A gondolier in traditional garb waits for his next customers—who almost certainly will be tourists. A spin under several of the city's 400 bridges runs about $50 an hour for up to five passengers. Residents, and visitors in a hurry or on a budget, usually walk or take water buses and water taxis to navigate the nearly 200 canals that wind among the city's 118 islands.

Photographer:

Ethan Hoffman, USA

● *Above*

Everything is ship-shape in the port of Genoa, Italy's fifth largest city. The 17-square-mile harbor is the largest in the country and claims Christopher Columbus as its most famous sailor.

Photographer:

Roberto Koch, Italy

● *Above*

The Amalfi coast south of Naples is known for its chic resorts, most notably the village of Positano, but fishing boats still sail from towns like Sorrento. Italy has more than 3,000 miles of coastline, which has made its borders difficult to defend but has also inspired a thriving fishing industry.

Photographer:
Michael Yamashita, USA

● *Right*

Net working: Mario De Agostini, 52, repairs a vital fishing tool in a seaside bar in the Sardinian port city of Cagliari. De Agostini, a factory worker by trade, often relaxes in the bar with his fisherman son, Antonio. Swordfish and tuna are plentiful in the waters off Cagliari, the largest city on the dry, rocky island that belonged by turns to Spain and to Austria prior to becoming part of the kingdom of Italy in 1861.

Photographer:
Peter Turnley, USA

● *Left*

All tracks lead to Rome or, to be more precise, to Stazione Termini, by far the largest and busiest of the capital's seven train stations. Like the major stations in Milan, Turin, Naples, Florence, Bologna, and Genoa, Rome's Termini is flooded with travelers for most of the day and evening. There are 31 daily trains between Rome and Milan alone, with the fastest, a nonstop, covering the 380 miles between Italy's two largest cities in just under four hours. Although Italy is smaller than California, it is criss-crossed by about 12,000 miles of railroad track.
Photographer:
Edoardo Fornaciari, Italy

● *Above*

A young man surveys the view out of a first class, non-smoking car at the Siena train station. Italian trains are divided into first and second class by comfort and seat width, with first class generally about 50 percent more expensive. A third class, which existed from the time Italy established the national train system in the late nineteenth century, was phased out in the 1960s.
Photographer:
Bradley E. Clift, USA

● *Left and above*

Several elegant ski resorts are nestled into the northwest corner of Italy near Courmayeur, in the region known as Valle d'Aosta. When they tire of working on their tans, well-heeled visitors to the area can avoid crowded ski lifts by hiring helicopters. Besides ferrying passengers, pilot Roberto d'Alessi (*right*) and co-pilot Dario Arzaroli also serve as an avalanche research team, monitoring the snow level and weather conditions in an attempt to predict where and when dangerous slides might occur.

Valle d'Aosta, where both French and Italian are official languages, is the smallest and least densely populated of Italy's 20 regions, and is one of four regions to enjoy a limited form of autonomy. The German-speaking Trentino-Alto Adige and the islands of Sardinia and Sicily are the other three.
Photographer:
Eric Lars Bakke, USA

● *Below*

Soldiers in the snow: Troops
from L'Aquila Battalion, Company 143 of Italy's elite alpine
military corps, the Alpini, train in
the Apennine mountains. Even
today, the Alpini play a significant role in the defense of a country whose northern border runs
among some of the highest and
steepest mountains in Europe.
Photographer:
Daniele Pellegrini, Italy

● *Left*

Two-year-old Andrea Avena plays bang-bang with his father Antonio, a brigadier in the carabinieri in the Calabrian town of Locri. Joining the carabinieri or other Italian police forces is often a way out of poverty for young men in the south, where industry remains relatively scarce and the arid, unforgiving land makes farming difficult. Antonio, 32, joined the carabinieri 12 years ago. While on duty, he usually carries the Beretta pistol held by his son.
Photographer:
Francesco Paolo Cito, Italy

● *Above*

Riot officers in training make their stand in Campochiaro, a village outside the provincial capital of Campobasso in Italy's Molise region. The trio are students at the nearby police school, where young men come to fulfill their year-long military obligation by training for four months and then serving as apprentices in the Polizia for eight months. 1989 saw an 8 percent increase in reported crimes over the year before, with murder, robbery, arson, and extortion on the rise, and kidnapping, drug trafficking, and crimes of sexual violence on the decline.
Photographer:
Mauro Vallinotto, Italy

● *Above, top*

Bettino Craxi, the outspoken
and energetic leader of Italy's
Socialist Party and perhaps the
country's most charismatic political figure, listens to a speaker
during a party meeting in
Genoa. Craxi became Italy's first
post-war Socialist prime minis-
ter in August, 1983 at the age
of 49, staying in the post until
1987—a remarkable achievement
in a country where since World
War II, governments have lasted
less than a year on average.
Photographer:
Roberto Koch, Italy

● *Above*

Digital communications: No-
where in the world is it more
true than in Italy that hands,
as Pope John Paul II wrote in a
1979 poem, "are the landscape
of the heart."
Photographer:
Doug Menuez, USA

Mayor Renzo Imbeni of the Partito Comunista Italiano takes to the streets to talk politics in Bologna, an affluent city of 420,000. Nationally, the fortunes of Imbeni's party—Italy's second-largest, after the Christian Democrats—have slipped since the mid-1970s, when one out of three Italians voted Communist. But 'Red Bologna' remains a stronghold of the PCI, which has ruled the city since the end of World War II. Imbeni doesn't have to worry about wasting his time talking to non-voters in his impromptu town meetings; usually close to 80 percent of voting-age Italians go to the polls on election day. *Photographer:* **Doug Menuez, USA**

● *Above*

The record room: A municipal clerk at the *anagrafe* searches through his files of birth, marriage, and death certificates as a crowd jams the tiny space outside his window. Italians who need copies of their records for any reason are obliged to make a trip to an anagrafe office, where the documents, like those at the Reggio di Calabria anagrafe pictured here, are often kept on small metal plates and stamped onto paper upon request.

Photographer:
Raphaël Gaillarde, France

● *Right*

Its narrow streets and alleys inaccessible to cars, the fishing village of Manarola is a walker's paradise. Local trains from La Spezia and Genoa provide transportation in and out of town; motorists have to leave their cars in the village's upper reaches. Manarola is also connected to four nearby villages by a hiking path, the Via dell'Amore, that follows the cliffs above the Ligurian Sea. Together, the five villages—Manarola, Riomaggiore, Corniglia, Vernazza, and Monterosso—are known as the Cinque Terre.

Photographer:
Joe Rossi, USA

● *Left and above*

Lifestyles of the rich and noble: Count Marco Emo Capodilista talks with his English wife Caroline in front of the Palladian villa near Treviso that has been in his family for more than 400 years. Homes built by Andrea Palladio, the master Renaissance architect whose work inspired Thomas Jefferson, dot the countryside of northeastern Italy. Among them, only Villa Emo is still inhabited by descendants of the original family. The count and countess live with their three children in what were originally the servants' quarters, preserving the bulk of the 300-foot-long villa as a museum—although they often entertain in the main ballroom (*above*) beneath frescoes painted by Giovanni Battista Zelotti in 1560.

Photographer:
Diego Goldberg, Argentina

● *Following page*

First comes love, then comes marriage, but fewer and fewer Italians are turning up in a baby carriage. The birth rate has dropped by half since the 1960s, to the point where families of seven or more now make up only about 1 percent of the population. In 1951 that figure was 12 percent.

Photographer:
Annie Griffiths Belt, USA

Annie Griffiths Belt

● *Left*

As *Day in the Life* photographer Jim Richardson discovered in Lecce, much of Italian life–from making pasta to playing with baby to sharing young secrets–takes place in the piazzas and streets. "There's so much public activity everywhere you go," marveled Richardson, "and it all seems so compressed–so intimate."
Photographer:
Jim Richardson, USA

● *Above*

Michela Carnevale serves pasta into a bowl held by her daughter, Lucia Masciotra. The two women make their own pasta by hand and serve it to family and friends each day on their small farm. While making pasta by hand is becoming less common in Italy, eating it is not: The average Italian consumes 65 pounds of pasta per year.

Photographer:
Nick Kelsh, USA

● *Right*

"I'm very strict about the family eating together," says Olindo Pelino, at the head of the lunch table in Sulmona. Like many Italians, family patriarch Pelino returns home from work in the early afternoon for *pranzo*, the biggest meal of the day. An Italian family's lunch typically includes a first course of pasta, soup or rice; a main course of meat or fish; a vegetable; and fruit, cheese, or dessert. After lunch and until about 3:30 PM, streets throughout the country are virtually empty, with shops shuttered and most people resting or spending time with their families. "The family is the most important thing in life," says Pelino, owner of a company that manufactures the candied almonds, or *confetti*, given out as party favors at family events such as baptisms, first communions, and weddings. "Without the family, you have nothing."

Photographer:
Stephanie Maze, USA

● *Following page*

Counting sheep does the trick for Tommaso Romani, a shepherd who takes his daily afternoon nap outside the Umbrian town of Trevi.

Photographer:
Bill Greene, USA

Bill Greene

On the rocks reclined, residents of Genoa enjoy *il dolce far niente*— the sweetness of doing nothing— in the afternoon sun.
Photographer:
Roberto Koch, Italy

● *Above and right*

Sisterly advice: At the Rosmini boarding school in Domodossola, 17-year-old Viviana Zuliani gets some pointers from Sister Gianfranca Puddu before hurrying off to the television room for the day's big event (*right*)— the 2:00 PM airing of *Quando Si Ama*, Italy's most popular soap opera. Viviana, who hopes to become a doctor, puts her studies aside to watch the show— a dubbed version of ABC-TV's *Loving* that draws 5 million Italian viewers a day.
Photographer:
Nicole Bengiveno, USA

● *Above*

St. Peter's Square and Basilica stand majestically at the end of one of Rome's widest streets, the Via della Conciliazione. The Via was begun in 1936 by Mussolini, who found the narrow streets between the church and the Tiber River to be too modest an approach to one of the world's most venerated buildings. In the right foreground is Castel Sant'Angelo, designed in A.D. 135 by the Emperor Hadrian as his tomb, and transformed during medieval times into a fortress. The elevated passageway from the Vatican to the Castel allowed Pope Clement VII to escape and hide during the sack of Rome in 1527.
Photographer:
Edoardo Fornaciari, Italy

● *Right*

The Papal ring: Some 13,000 calls a day come into the Vatican, where Sister Yolanda Arenas, Sister Elsy Kattiparampil, and Sister Alma Liberia share switchboard duties with nine other multilingual nuns. While many callers need to be connected with one of the offices or residences in the 108-acre Vatican City, others call for tourist or religious information. And then there are the messages for the Pope: The switchboard logged more than 50,000 calls on December 22, 1989, with the great majority simply wanting to wish His Holiness a merry Christmas.
Photographer:
Don Doll, S.J., USA

Don Doll, S.J.

● *Previous page*

The largest Catholic church in the world, St. Peter's Basilica dominates Vatican City and serves as the spiritual center of the world's 900 million Catholics. Construction of the 600-foot by 450-foot basilica, built on the site of earlier churches bearing the name of St. Peter, was begun in 1506 and completed in 1626. The dome was designed by Michelangelo, whose famed sculpture, the *Pietà*, sits behind bulletproof glass in a much-visited corner of the church.
Photographer:
Don Doll, S.J., USA

● *Left and above*

The spiritual leader of the Roman Catholic Church and head of state of the world's smallest country, Città del Vaticano, Pope John Paul II greets Portugal's President Mario Soares and his wife Maria de Jesus Barroso Soares. In a typical year *Il Papa* receives hundreds of distinguished visitors, including about two dozen heads of state. Other pilgrims make do with "semi-private" audiences with His Holiness, who often receives five or six such groups a day. Official Vatican photographers attempt to capture his every handshake; later, precious souvenirs of the event go on sale (*above*) for between 4,000 and 6,000 lire, or about $3 to $5, depending on size.
Photographer:
Don Doll, S.J., USA

● *Above*

The Pope's coat of arms gets a touch-up in the Vatican Gardens. Each of the 251 popes since the third century has had his own coat of arms; the "M" in John Paul II's is for Mary, the mother of Jesus, and the keys represent the keys to St. Peter's Basilica.

Photographer:
Don Doll, S.J., USA

● *Right*

"When they die," an Italian proverb says, "they are all saints." On her daily trip to Asolo's local cemetery to water the flowers at the graves of her sainted friends, whose snapshots adorn their tombs, 89-year-old Domenica Rinaldo consented to a portrait by *Day in the Life* photographer Annie Griffiths Belt on one condition. "Please send me a copy of the picture," she said, "so they can put it on my grave when I die."

Photographer:
Annie Griffiths Belt, USA

● *Following page*

A soccer shrine on a Naples street: The black-bordered announcement, in the style of funeral announcements often posted in public places, reports the death of Milan, "after a long season of agony," and offers "the most sincere condolences" from the fans of Napoli—the Naples team that overtook Milan in the season's final weeks to win the 1989-1990 *scudetto*, the Italian soccer championship. The framed photo is of Diego Armando Maradona, Napoli's Argentine-born star, who is generally considered to be the world's best player.

Photographer:
Bruno Barbey, France

2:45 PM

Bruno Barbey

Above

Taking a break from his duties
behind the counter at the family
salumeria, Adriano Doria shows
his grandson Fabio the moves
that made him a minor-league
soccer player in the years before
World War II. "We make the
best prosciutto in the whole
country," says Adriano of the
grocery store he opened in
1951 in his hometown of
Domodossola–just a short corner kick from the Swiss border.
Photographer:
Nicole Bengiveno, USA

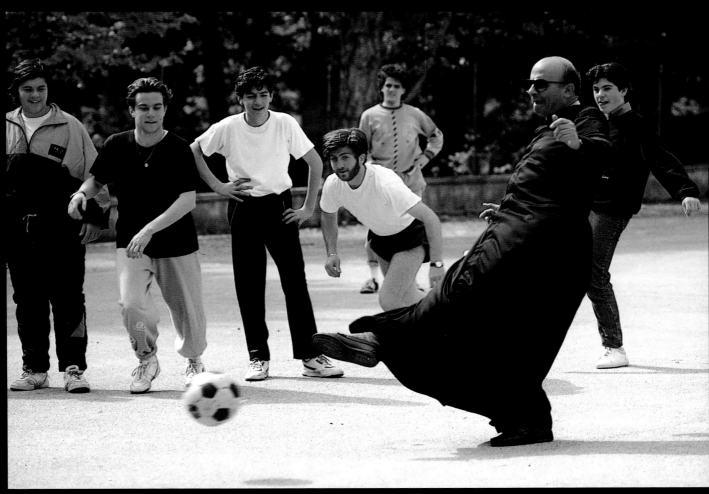

● *Above*

Look goalward, angel: Putting
his best foot forward, Don Luigi
Rancitelli shares a game of *calcio*
with young members of his
parish in the mountain town of
Sulmona. The 57-year-old priest
also plays volleyball with his
young charges, and says of his
athletic career: "At my age, I can't
play every day, but I try to get
out there as much as possible."
Photographer:
Stephanie Maze, USA

● *Above*

Just for kicks: Batman and his pals take a break from soccer practice in Nettuno. About 2 million Italians are members of officially registered soccer teams, and millions more spend Sunday afternoons either watching games in person or following their progress on TV or radio.
Photographer:
Gary Matoso, USA

● *Right*

The preferred participatory sport of Italy's post-soccer set is bocce, which historians trace to a game played by Roman soldiers during the Punic Wars in the third century B.C. Where the soliders used stones, more modern bocce is played with balls, which competitors roll in an attempt to get as close as possible to a smaller ball, or *pallino*. Italy has won all four world championships sponsored by the International Bocce Confederation and will soon have a chance to compete for the world bocce crown on a larger stage: The ancient game has been named a demonstration sport for the 1992 Summer Olympics in Barcelona.
Photographer:
Annie Griffiths Belt, USA

● *Above*

Pedal pushers: Cyclists from 20 nations race through the countryside near Viterbo, about 50 miles north of Rome, on the second day of the Giro delle Regioni. To shoot the Giro, which is sponsored by the Communist Party's daily newspaper *l'Unità*, photographer Jim Mendenhall strapped himself to the back of a motorcycle just in front of the lead riders. Cycling, auto racing, and basketball are Italy's most popular spectator sports—after, of course, soccer.
Photographer:
Jim Mendenhall, USA

● *Right*

With a world-famous bridge for a backdrop, four members of the Società Canottieri Firenze—the Florence Rowing Club—work out on the Arno River. The Ponte Vecchio, or Old Bridge, dates back to 1345, and was the only bridge in Florence not destroyed by retreating Nazi troops in 1944. The Ponte Vecchio's shops, once occupied by butchers, have been the almost exclusive domain of jewelers and goldsmiths for 400 years.
Photographer:
Guglielmo de' Micheli, Italy

● *Above*

Living by the sword: Two knights in modern armor thrust and parry at the National Fencing Championships in Lamezia Terme. In the 1988 Summer Olympics in Seoul, Italy's Stefano Cerioni won the gold medal in the individual foil competition; Italian fencers also won the silver in the women's team foil and the bronze in the men's team sabre.

Photographer:

Robb Kendrick, USA

● *Right*

Fourteen years after he first decided he wanted to be a professional baseball player, 22-year-old Fernando Ricci is the *ricevitore*, or catcher, for the Nettuno club in the 16-team Italian league. Although baseball is relatively popular in Nettuno, where it was introduced by U.S. troops during World War II, it remains very much a minor sport in the rest of the country. Most players earn only about $10,000 for the season, which lasts from April to September and features three games a week; the two American players each team is allowed usually earn substantially more.

Photographer:

Doug Menuez, USA

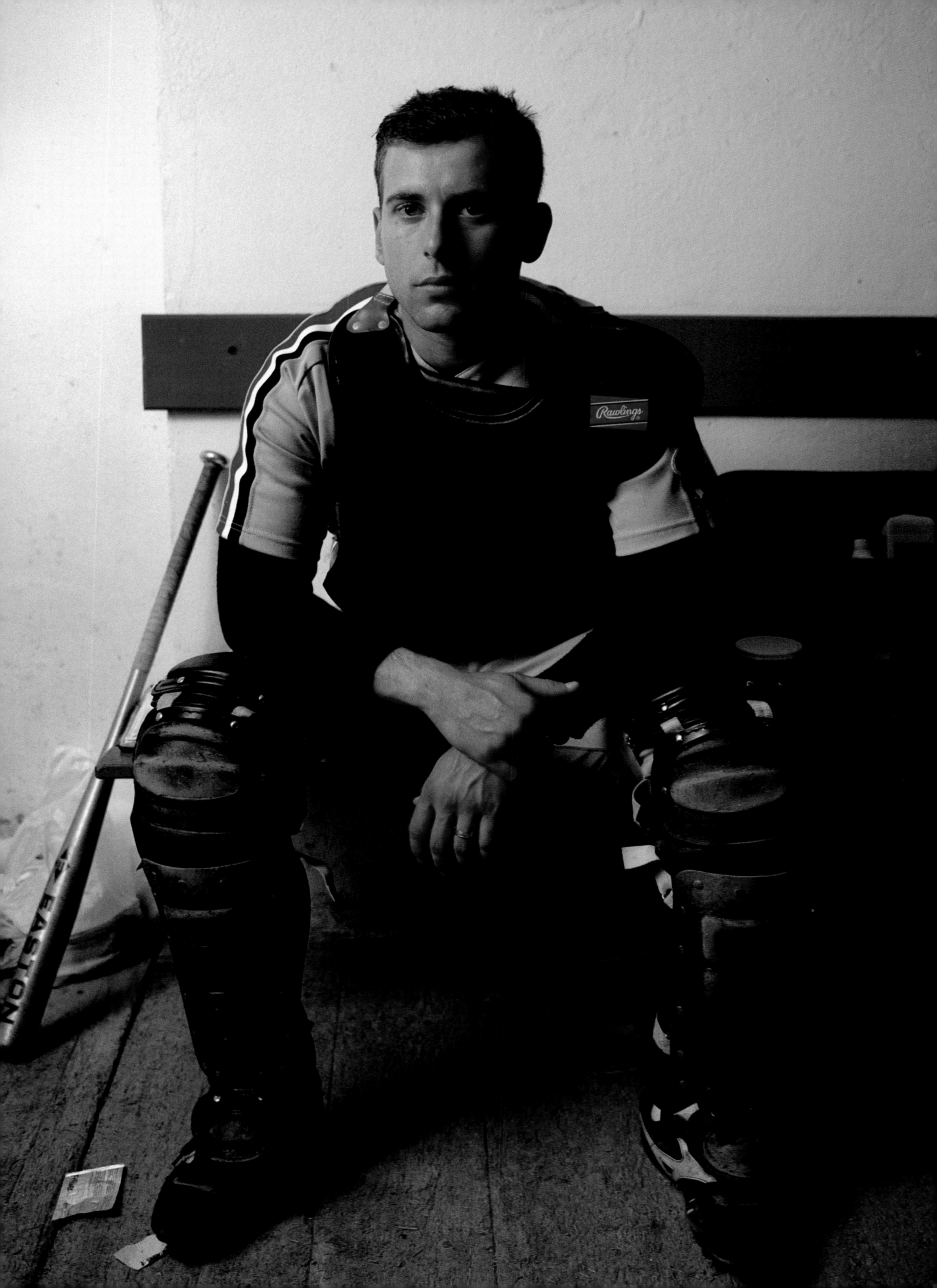

● *Left*

A human tide rolls down Via Condotti, named after the underground conduits that were part of ancient Rome's extensive series of aqueducts. Two thousand years later, Via Condotti–seen here from atop the nearby Spanish Steps–is awash in high fashion, with stores like Valentino, Bulgari, Gucci, Sergio Valente, Ferragamo, and Battistoni making it the capital's premier shopping street.
Photographer:
Paul Chesley, USA

● *Above*

Moto mania: Italy's narrow streets and expensive gasoline– about four dollars a gallon–make it the perfect place for motorcycles and motor scooters, the roar of which has become as much a part of Italian city life as red wine and stray cats.
Photographer:
Edoardo Fornaciari, Italy

● *Left*

Four boys in Rome's Piazza di Spagna show that little has changed in the land of love since the days of the medieval French king Charles V, who said, "I speak Spanish to God, French to men, German to horses, and Italian to women."
Photographer:
Mike Davis, USA

● *Above*

O sole mio: April 27, 1990, was clear and bright in Rome, thanks perhaps to Jupiter, the Roman god responsible for controlling the weather. The capital enjoys more than 270 sunny days each year.
Photographer:
Paul Chesley, USA

● *Above*

"Mosiacs are becoming a lost art," says Michele Galluzzi, 19, a student at Ravenna's Istituto Statale d'Arte Mosaico. Italian students choose between seven different kinds of high schools: scientific, classical, vocational, technical, teacher training, foreign language, and artistic. Galluzzi, who likes riding his motorcycle, reading Edgar Allan Poe, and listening to The Ramones, is one of the 3 percent of students who at-

tend an academy of fine arts. Galluzzi left his hometown of Rimini to study in Ravenna, once capital of the Roman Empire and still renowned for its Byzantine mosaics.
Photographer:
Randy Olson, USA

● *Right*

University of Bologna students check their calculations in the chemistry library at Europe's oldest university, where the astronomer Copernicus and the writers Dante, Petrarch, and Tasso once attended classes. About 275,000 first-year students enroll at universities throughout Italy annually, but only 80,000 stay on to graduate. Fittingly for the country that gave the world the Renaissance, arts and literature degrees are the most prevalent, accounting for one-fifth of Italy's university graduates each year.
Photographer:
Robin Moyer, USA

● *Left*

Sit-in, Italian style: University students at the Brera Academy of Fine Arts in Milan lend their support to a wave of protests that have taken place throughout the country by occupying Academy buildings. Protests began at many of Italy's 50 universities in January, 1990 and continued through the spring, with students rallying against a proposed law that would allow corporations to help finance the overcrowded and bureaucratic university system. Some 180,000 students are enrolled at the La Sapienza campus of the University of Rome alone.

Photographer:

Elliott Erwitt, USA

● *Above*

Overcrowding is a fact of life in Naples, even on motor scooters. Official figures give the city's population as 1.2 million, but some unofficial estimates have pegged the figure at twice that. And for all those people, there are too few jobs. The decline of the steel industry has hit Naples hard, as has competition in shipping from other southern ports—driving thousands of breadwinners into sweatshops and other sources of illegal employment.

Photographer:

Letizia Battaglia, Italy

Body heat: the water is always 98.6 degrees at the thermal baths in Saturnia, halfway between Rome and Florence, where for 3,000 years visitors have come in search of a cure for what ails them. The luxurious Terme di Saturnia resort hotel bills itself as an "Institute of Esthetic Medicine"; a mile or so down the road, at the so-called *terme dei poveri*, or poor people's baths, tourists Patricia Vleti, Arianna Guerra, and Markus Zimmerman take advantage of a waterfall at a collection of natural pools open free to the public.
Photographer:
Jay Dickman, USA

Ballerinas in training check their posture under the watchful eye of British teacher Carol Watson at the Palestra La Torre in Ravenna. The school, one of several in the city of 135,000, offers classes for girls of all ages, starting with the four- and five-year-olds pictured here.
Photographer:
Randy Olson, USA

Through the eyes of children: Kodak gave some 200 Italian kids S100EF autofocus cameras with which to participate in **A Day in the Life of Italy** on April 27, 1990. Here is a selection of the best images from the 400 rolls taken by Italy's photojournalists of the future.

Stefano Boriosi, 10, Rome

Massimo Belli, 9, Rome

Federico Durantini, 10, Rome

Federica Pacioni, 10, Rome

Sabrina Tramentozzi, 10, Rome

Annabella Donà, 10, Assisi

Antonello Fontebasso, 10, Rome

Francesco Gianolla, 13, Trieste

Alessio Ramassotti, 10, Rome

Alessandro D'Agostino, 9, Brescia

● *Above*

With colors reminiscent of a Titian masterpiece, even ice cream is a work of art in Italy, where *gelato* is a national passion.
Photographer:
Jim Mendenhall, USA

● *Right*

Visiting dad at work is all the sweeter when his job is running the family pastry shop, as six-year-old Carlo Maria Balzola discovers every day after school. The Pasticceria Balzola was founded in Alassio by Carlo's grandfather in 1902. The family lives upstairs from the shop in a fourteenth-century building that also houses the factory where the candies and pastries are made. "Eating sweets is a family vice," says Carlo's father, Pasquale. "If we were diabetics, we'd all be dead."
Photographer:
Vittoriano Rastelli, Italy

The old school cafeteria was never like this: Among the rewards of student life for boarders at Domodossola's Rosmini School are the desserts made by hand by Sister Paulina Venefrida. Rosmini's pleasures don't come cheap, with tuition and room and board running about $5,000 a year. But the potential payoff is great: Three-quarters of the students who pass through Rosmini's halls—and Sister Venefrida's kitchen—go on to university.
Photographer:
Nicole Bengiveno, USA

● A grocery store shelf in Palermo. *Photographer:* **David C. Turnley, USA**

● Outside an operating room in Milan. *Photographer:* **Bill Pierce, USA**

• *Above*

Noodlin' around: The center-piece of the Italian diet rolls down the line at the largest pasta factory in the world, the Barilla plant in Parma. A thousand tons of pasta are produced here each day, for domestic use as well as for export to 56 countries; the United States alone imports about 60,000 tons of Italian pasta a year. Spaghetti is Barilla's biggest seller, but the company's eight factories throughout Italy turn out 120 other types of pasta as well.

Photographer:

Joe McNally, USA

• *Right*

Say cheese: Wheels of Parmigiano Reggiano—what Americans call parmesan cheese—are cured in a cooling room, where temperatures hover at about 60 degrees Fahrenheit with relative humidity of 85 percent. This year-long process is part of a two-year journey that turns skimmed cow's milk into the hard, fragrant cheese that Italians are just as likely to eat in chunks as to sprinkle on pasta. The several varieties of Italian hard cheese made from cow's milk are known, collectively, as *grana*; Parmigiano Reggiano, the production of which is closely monitored for authenticity by government inspectors, is the highest quality, and sells in Italy for about $9.50 a pound.

Photographer:

Joe McNally, USA

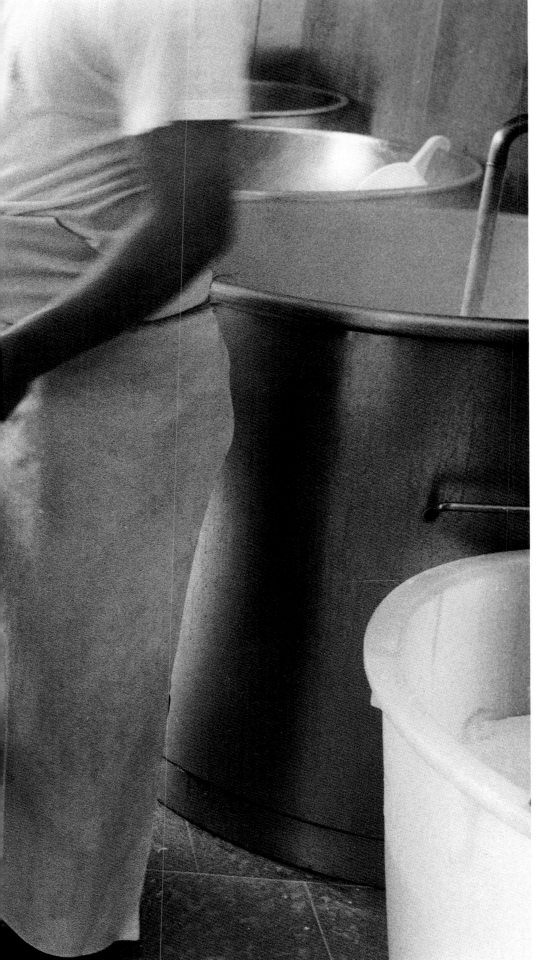

● *Left*

Practiced hands stir and strain
to turn water buffalo milk into
a prized cheese in about nine
hours at the Azienda Bonanno
e Bodda, in Italy's mozzarella region. About 500 water buffalo
live on Bonanno e Bodda land
outside the town of Fondi.
Cheese connoisseurs turn up
their noses at cow mozzarella,
insisting that only *mozzarella di
bufala*, produced in the coastal
flatlands between Rome and
Naples, is worthy of use in
pizza, pasta sauces, and the de-
lectable *insalata caprese*–slices of
tomato and fresh mozzarella,
with basil sprinkled on top.
Photographer:
John Loengard, USA

● *Left and above*

Despite the fact that about 80 percent of Italy's terrain is classified as hilly or mountainous, the industrious Italians have always found ways to farm their land. Today, more than half of the country's land is devoted to agriculture, most of it in farms smaller than 12 acres. Farm production has risen in recent years, but agriculture's importance in the continually diversifying Italian economy has shrunk; where agriculture accounted for about one-fifth of the gross domestic product in 1960, it now accounts for about one-twentieth. Italy is the European Community's leading producer of fruits and vegetables, led by grapes, olives, and citrus fruits; wheat is the principal grain crop, followed by corn and rice.

Photographer:

Georg Gerster, Switzerland

Their branches a sign of peace and their fruit hailed as a gift from the heavens, olive trees cover much of the hilly terrain in Liguria, a region on Italy's northwest coast. With the village of Valloria in the background, Pietro Balbo prunes one of the trees whose fruit produces the oil considered so important that its classification into four categories–from the premium Extravirgin all the way down to the more pedestrian Virgin–is tightly regulated by the Italian government. Millions of dollars' worth is exported each year, including about three-quarters of the olive oil sold in the United States.
Photographer:
Vittoriano Rastelli, Italy

Scenery reminiscent of *The Sound of Music* lends a Teutonic touch to Italy's northernmost region, outside the town known to most Italians as Bressanone. Locals are more likely to call the town by its German name, Brixen, since two-thirds of the 450,000 people in the surrounding province of Bolzano speak German as their native tongue. Bolzano and the province to its south, Trent, form the region now known as Trentino-Alto Adige, and were bounced between various Austrian and Italian rulers for centuries before becoming part of Italy in the spoils of World War I. Some residents of the region have never accepted the 1918 border, however, and consider themselves Austrians.
Photographer:
Rick Rickman, USA

Rick Rickman

● *Right*

Ignoring an ancient tradition that discourages getting married on a Friday–the day that Christ was crucified–a bride and groom descend one of the many stone stairways connecting the hills and the sea in Naples, the boisterous southern port that is Italy's third-largest city.

Photographer:

Letizia Battaglia, Italy

Following page

That's *amore*: from the ritual peck on each cheek that serves as both greeting and farewell, to the spontaneous buss of affection shared unselfconsciously by adults of the same sex, to the passionate public embrace of lovers of all ages, Italians are frequent practitioners of *il bacio*– the kiss.

Naples. Photographer: **Bruno Barbey, France**

Ravenna. Photographer: **Randy Olson, USA**

Rome. Photographer: **Paul Chesley, USA**

Eggi. Photographer: **Bill Greene, USA**

Rome. Photographer: **Paul Chesley, USA**

Trieste. Photographer: **Misha Erwitt, USA**

● *Above*

Poldo and Livia Romagnoli in a
beach cabin in Porto San Giorgio, one of dozens of resorts on
the Adriatic coast that together
play host to an estimated 3 million visitors every summer.
Photographer:
Patrick Tehan, USA

● *Above*

A couple at their home in Bari, a port city ruled at various times by Greeks, Romans, Goths, Lombards, Byzantines, and Normans.
Photographer:
Enrico Bossan, Italy

● *Left*

Grandfather and grandson catch up on their reading on a Rome street. Forty years ago, with Italy still rebuilding its schools and mass communications after twenty years of fascism and five years of world war, about 10 percent of the country's adult men and 15 percent of the adult women were illiterate. Now, only about 2 percent of Italian men and about 4 percent of Italian women are unable to read.
Photographer:
Steve McCurry, USA

● *Above*

Afternoons in the piazza are the perfect time for old friends, like these men in Lucca, to have a drink, a cup of coffee, or a glass of mineral water while catching up on gossip or debating the relative merits of the latest Italian government.
Photographer:
Dilip Mehta, Canada

A happy father holds his son on a Naples street decorated to celebrate the title won by Napoli, the local team, in the 18-team Italian national soccer league. Soccer is big business in Italy, where salaries exceeding $1 million a year lure the world's best players, and where fans place about $4 billion worth of legal and illegal bets on the outcome of each Sunday's games. Regional pride, still strong in a country that became politically unified only 120 years ago, fuels the passion that rocks stadiums—and occasionally spills over into violence—throughout the country.
Photographer:
Letizia Battaglia, Italy

● *Left*

Every day's a saint's day in Italy. In the Tuscan city of Lucca, April 27 belongs to Santa Zita, patron saint of housewives. Families visit the medieval Basilica of San Frediano to honor the thirteenth-century saint, who is said to have been a housekeeper for a rich Luccan family. One day, while taking some bread to the poor, she was stopped by her employer, who angrily asked what she was carrying in her apron. When she opened the apron to show him, the bread had turned to flowers.
Photographer:
Dilip Mehta, Canada

● *Above*

Mamma's boy: Home on break, Alberto Pallotta, 31, gives his mother a squeeze before heading back to his job as a conductor for the state railroad on the run from Domodossola to Milan. Italy's high youth unemployment rate and chronic housing shortage have combined with tradition to keep nearly 90 percent of Italians living with their parents through their mid-twenties. And almost a third of the country's men still live at home at age 34. "Of course Alberto lives with us," says his mother, Libana. "He's still young, and he's not married yet."
Photographer:
Nicole Bengiveno, USA

● *Following page*

Modern graffiti meets Gothic majesty in Milan, where the 135 spires of Europe's second-largest cathedral reach skyward in this view from a neighboring building. About 40,000 worshipers can fit into the Duomo at one time. Construction on the church began in 1386 and was finished in 1813 on orders from Napoleon, who was then ruling Milan.
Photographer:
Elliott Erwitt, USA

Elliott Erwitt

Enrico Bossan

● *Previous page*

Wearing robes designed to show their devotion to Mary Magdalene, school boys in the village of Bitetto take part in a procession for the feast day of Beato Giacomo Varinger. Varinger, a local Franciscan lay brother, was beatified in 1700, putting him just a papal proclamation away from sainthood. Local priests have chosen this year, the 500th anniversary of Varinger's death, to push their campaign for his canonization.

Photographer:

Enrico Bossan, Italy

● *Left*

Father knows best: A priest hears confession at a church in Lucca. Catholics are expected to confess their serious sins to a priest at least once a year, although many go to confession far more frequently. According to church law as interpreted by the Fourth Lateran Council in 1215, anyone hearing a confession—whether priest, bystander, or interpreter—is bound to secrecy.

Photographer:

Dilip Mehta, Canada

● *Above*

Pilgrims pray before the tomb of Padre Pio de Pietralcina, a priest who died in 1968 after spending 50 years in a sixteenth-century monastery in San Giovanni Rotondo. Today there are more than 20 hotels in the small town catering to the faithful who come to honor the priest. Padre Pio, it is said, often appeared in two places at once, and also had the stigmata—bleeding, like Christ on the cross, from his hands, feet, and side.

Photographer:

Seny Norasingh, Laos

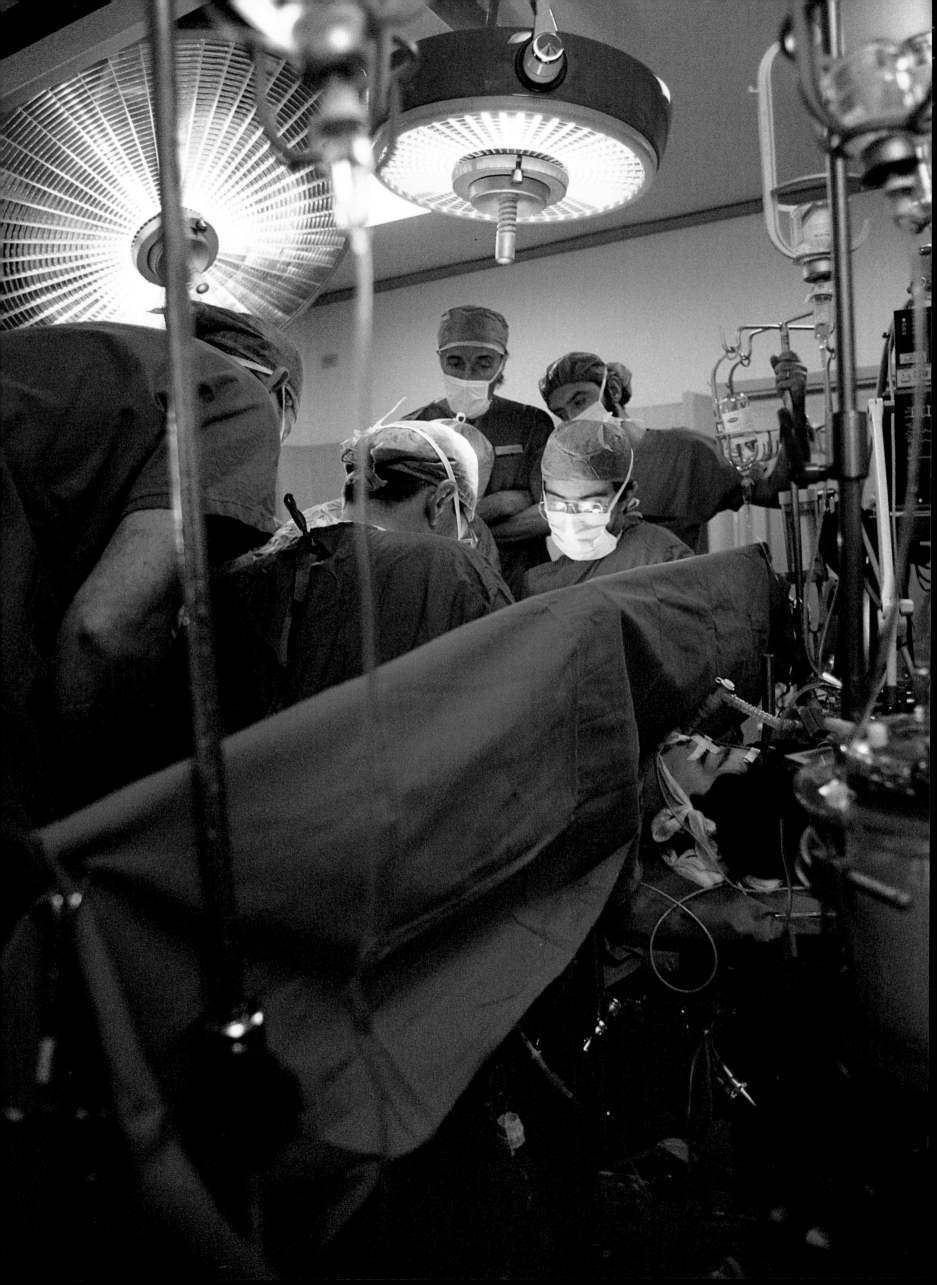

● *Left and above*

A team of surgeons works to save a life by replacing a 12-year-old boy's liver at the country's leading transplant facility, the Ospedale Policlinico Maggiore in Milan. Because of a shortage of donors and an archaic, paperwork-laden system of approving transplants and matching donors to recipients, Italy ranks far behind most other Western European nations in the annual number of organ transplants; a bill to speed up the process has languished in Parliament for 10 years. Says chief transplant surgeon Luigi Rainero Fassati, shown recuperating after the 14-hour operation, "Our government will spend millions on a new soccer stadium, while our medical facilities are falling apart." The 53-year-old Fassati has performed 103 liver transplants in his career, including two on women who have gone on to have children. "If the operation is successful," he says, "I feel like I have breathed life into someone. It is incredibly uplifting."
Photographer:
Bill Pierce, USA

● Above and right

A nineteenth-century priest's dream is a reality at the Little House of Divine Providence, home to more than a thousand Third World refugees and mentally or physically disabled people. Giuseppe Benedetto Cottolengo founded La Piccola Casa della Divina Provvidenza on the outskirts of Turin in 1832, 10 years before his death; it is now the hub of an international charitable organization, with facilities in Africa, the United States, and several European countries. For his devotion to the sick and homeless, Father Cottolengo was proclaimed a saint in 1934 by Pope Pius XI.
Photographer:
Mary Ellen Mark, USA

● Following page

Rome's afternoon sun streams into the Pantheon through the *oculus,* an opening that represents the all-seeing eye of heaven. Architecturally, the Pantheon, or "temple of all the gods," is as close to perfect as mortals can come: The dome's diameter, 142 feet, is exactly the same as its height from the floor. Except for the addition of various tombs, including those of Italy's royal family and the Renaissance master Raphael, the Pantheon has changed very little since the Emperor Hadrian built it, on the site of an earlier Roman temple, between A.D. 120 and 125. Nearly 500 years later, Pope Boniface IV added an altar and consecrated it as a Christian Church. It wasn't until 1960, with the construction of the Palazzo dello Sport for the Rome Olympics, that a larger dome was built anywhere in the world.
Photographer:
Paul Chesley, USA

Paul Chesley

● *Left*

Although poverty remains a problem in Italy, especially in the south, the country has been transformed in the twentieth century from a poor agricultural land to a prosperous industrial country. Life expectancy serves as one index: When Maria Carmina Iaconelli, seen here at her home in San Biagio Saracinisco, was born in 1900, life expectancy at birth for Italians was only 43 years. Italian girls born in the 1980s can expect to live an average of 78 years, while life expectancy for boys born in the same decade is 71.

Photographer:

Jerry Valente, USA

● *Above*

Vendors wait for a sale in Cosenza, a provincial capital in Italy's poorest region, Calabria. Over the last century, more than a million Calabrese have left the mountains and valleys of their native region in search of work elsewhere—in northern Italy, northern Europe, or the Americas.

Photographer:

Robb Kendrick, USA

Antonio Rossi and his grandson Giovanni Paollilo in San Biagio Saracinisco, Lazio. Photographer: **Jerry Valente, USA**

Celeste Del Basso and her granddaughter Celestina in Agnone, Molise. Photographer: **Nick Kelsh, USA**

● *Left*

It's a count's life for Neri Capponi, a lawyer for the Vatican, whose ancestors came to Florence from Orvieto in 1215 and became nobility in 1701. In modern, democratic Italy, the title 'count' is purely honorific, but Capponi, here in the drawing room of the 580-year-old family home, wears it proudly.
Photographer:
Guglielmo de' Micheli, Italy

● *Above*

The late afternoon glow crowns a shopper in Parma, a provincial capital of 175,000 in the affluent region of Emilia-Romagna.
Photographer:
Joe McNally, USA

● *Right*

Fire man: In the centuries-old tradition of Italian street artists who have used the piazza as their stage, Roberto Boscolo shows a hot time to a crowd in Perugia during *passeggiata*, the traditional early evening walk.
Photographer:
Melissa Farlow, USA

● *Following page*

The building that Romans love to hate, the blindingly white Vittoriano, dominates this view from the top of the dome of St. Peter's Basilica in the Vatican. Officially known as the Victor Emmanuel Monument and constructed to honor unified Italy's first king, the monument is more commonly known as "The Wedding Cake" or "The Typewriter." Work on the monument began in 1885 and finished in 1911, with the tomb of an unknown soldier added after World War I.
Photographer:
Don Doll, S.J., USA

Don Doll, S.J.

Bill Greene

● *Previous page*

Follow the leader: A flock of
sheep heads for home in the
hills of Umbria, a region often
called the Green Heart of Italy.
Photographer:
Bill Greene, USA

● *Below*

The workday finally over, rush-
hour traffic in Florence snakes
along the Arno and over two
of the eight bridges that cross
the river within the city limits.
About a half-million people live
in Florence, but traffic is exacer-
bated by the 5 million tourists
who visit the city each year.
Photographer:
Logan Bentley, USA

● *Left*

It's dinnertime at the Carnevale
household, and the family
shares its pasta and wine with
several forest rangers—identifi-
able by their gray sweaters
with green arm stripes—who
were working nearby.
Photographer:
Nick Kelsh, USA

● *Above*

In the kitchen of the Chianti
Valley's Villa Miranda Hotel,
Lido Bensi enjoys a snack while
fellow cook Pia Scarpetti cuts
pasta dough for *tagliatelle*. The
38-room hotel is the center-
piece of a 170-acre working
farm which produces all of the
food consumed by its guests,
including red wine, virgin olive
oil, and honey.
Photographer:
Sarah Leen, USA

Claus C. Meyer

● *Previous pages 184-85*

The bell tower of San Giorgio Maggiore, bearing a strong resemblance to its more famous cousin in nearby St. Mark's Square, rises from the Venetian island of San Giorgio.
Photographer:
Claus C. Meyer, Germany

● *Previous pages 186-87*

Daylight gives way to evening in the medieval village of Scanno, nestled in the mountains of south-central Italy.
Photographer:
Stephanie Maze, USA

● *Below*

The flooded fields glimmer at sunset near Vercelli, in the heart of Italy's rice-producing region. Fields throughout the area are flushed with water each spring for a few weeks, then drained so that the rice seedlings can take root. The fields are then flooded again, and stay under water until just before the September harvest.
Photographer:
Marcello Bertinetti, Italy

● *Above and right*

Opera star Giuseppe Sabbatini gets a final touch-up before going on stage at Parma's Teatro Regio to sing the lead tenor's role in *Werther*, a work composed by the Frenchman Jules Massenet in 1892. As a musical form, opera dates back to the late sixteenth and early seventeenth centuries, with the first opera generally considered to be Jacopo Peri's *Daphne* in 1597. While Venice and Rome were the early centers of world opera, the two cities were eclipsed in importance by Milan and its Teatro alla Scala in the nineteenth century, thanks in large part to the genius of composer Giuseppe Verdi. But opera's popularity in Italy is not limited to large, world-class cities; provincial capitals are justifiably proud of opera houses like the Teatro Regio, which was built in 1829 and is a regular stop for virtually every major opera production that tours the country. *Photographer:*
Joe McNally, USA

• *Right*

The red blues: Emanuele Raga-
nato listens to a speaker at a
Communist Party rally in Lecce.
Six weeks earlier, delegates to
the party's convention in Bologna had voted by a 2-1 margin
for sweeping changes in both
substance and style for what has
long been the West's largest
communist party—changes op-
posed by many in the party's
traditional base, the industrial
working class. By the end of
1990, a new name was to have
been chosen, as a key symbol of
the party's strategy to reach out
to environmentalists, civil liber-
tarians, feminists, and other
non-communists generally considered to fall toward the left of
the Italian political spectrum.
Photographer:
Jim Richardson, USA

● *Left*

Bright lights, big appetite: On a cobblestoned street in Rome, a *ristorante* and an *osteria* beckon the hungry.
Photographer:
Don Doll, S.J., USA

● *Above*

The streets of Bitetto are lit up in celebration of the feast day of the fifteenth-century Franciscan brother Beato Giacomo Varinger. The town of 9,000 holds the festival annually, a ritual of feasts, fireworks, and entertainment.
Photographer:
Enrico Bossan, Italy

● *Left*

Boys will be girls: Born as males, Milan residents Claudia Preda, Gabriella Nobile, and Alessandra Di Stefano have taken on female names, and are in the process of hormone treatments in anticipation of gender-change surgery. They'll have to go abroad for the operations, which are illegal in Italy; according to the Boston-based International Foundation for Gender Education, Belgium is the destination of choice for Italians seeking a new gender.
Photographer:
Dana Fineman, USA

● *Above*

Shady business: A Senegalese street merchant pleads his case at the marketplace in Florence's Loggia del Porcellino. Much has changed since the poet Percy Bysshe Shelley called Italy a "paradise of exiles" in 1818: Racism of an increasingly violent nature has plagued the country in recent years, as some 100,000 immigrants—60 percent of them Africans—enter the country each year, most of them illegally. The country's emergence as a target for mass immigration contrasts starkly with the pattern that prevailed throughout most of the twentieth century. Between 1900 and 1920, nearly 3 million Italians emigrated to the United States in search of a better life, with millions more leaving their homeland in subsequent years for Australia, South America, Canada, and northern Europe.
Photographer:
Dino Fracchia, Italy

● *Above*

Couch potatoes: A couple at a Modena disco sit one out to attend to some affairs of the heart.
Photographer:
George Steinmetz, USA

● *Right*

Friday night fever in Milan, the dance capital of a dance-crazy country. Concerned about the growing use of psychedelic drugs in discotheques and a rash of early-morning drunk-driving incidents involving disco patrons, the government recently set a 2:00 AM closing time for all dance halls except those in tourist areas, which may stay open until 4:00 AM. About 20 percent of the money Italians spend on entertainment is spent in discos.
Photographer:
Dana Fineman, USA

● *Following page*

Roman holiday: thrill-seekers on a whirl at Luna Park. Opened in 1960, Rome's largest amusement park—like many others in Italy—borrows its name from one at Coney Island.
Photographer:
Paul Chesley, USA

Paul Chesley

9:00 PM: An estimated 80,000 Gypsies, like this family in
Sardinia, constitute the most mistrusted minority group in Italy.
Photographer: **Peter Turnley, USA**

10:00 PM: Disco patrons dance the night away in Modena,
a city of 175,000 people in Emilia-Romagna.
Photographer: George Steinmetz, USA

12:00 AM: The long day's journey of 100 photographers ends in
Florence, Renaissance heart of an ancient land and modern nation.
Photographer: **Guglielmo de' Micheli, Italy**

Doug Menuez

Photographers' Assignment Locations

Photographers from all over the world traveled to Rome on Pan American World Airways for their shoot on April 27, 1990. Our special thanks go to Pan Am; their 50 years of unrivaled experience in flying to Europe ensured the success of this unique adventure.

Judy Griesedieck, San Remo

1 Eddie Adams
2 Monica Almeida
3 Lexine M. Alpert
4 Livio Anticoli
5 Eric Lars Bakke
6 Bruno Barbey
7 Letizia Battaglia
8 Ernesto Bazan
9 Nicole Bengiveno
10 Logan Bentley
11 P.F. Bentley
12 Gianni Berengo Gardin
13 Marcello Bertinetti
14 Enrico Bossan
15 Torin Boyd
16 Marilyn Bridges
17 Michael Bryant
18 René Burri
19 Bill Cafer Jr.
20 Romano Cagnoni
21 Elisabetta Catalano
22 Paul Chesley
23 Francesco Paolo Cito
24 Bradley E. Clift
25 Pedro Coll
26 Mike Davis
27 Ricardo DeAratanha
28 Mario De Biasi
29 Guglielmo de' Micheli
30 Jay Dickman
31 Don Doll, S.J.
32 John Dominis
33 Elliott Erwitt
34 Misha Erwitt
35 Melissa Farlow

36 Robert Fasulo
37 Franco Ferraris
38 Dana Fineman
39 Franco Fontana
40 Edoardo Fornaciari
41 Dino Fracchia
42 Rudi Frey
43 J.W. Fry
44 Raphaël Gaillarde
45 Sam Garcia
46 Georg Gerster
47 Gianni Giansanti
48 Diego Goldberg
49 Lynn Goldsmith
50 Bill Greene
51 Judy Griesedieck
52 Annie Griffiths Belt
53 Volker Hinz
54 Ethan Hoffman
55 Mark Kauffman
56 Nick Kelsh
57 Robb Kendrick
58 Roberto Koch
59 Steve Krongard
60 Jean-Pierre Laffont
61 Sarah Leen
62 Silvia Lelli
63 Andy Levin
64 Barry Lewis
65 John Loengard
66 Gerd Ludwig
67 Mary Ellen Mark
68 John Marmaras
69 Richard Marshall
70 Nico Marziali
71 Roberto Masotti

72 Gary Matoso
73 Stephanie Maze
74 Steve McCurry
75 Joe McNally
76 Dilip Mehta
77 Marcello Mencarini
78 Jim Mendenhall
79 Doug Menuez
80 Claus C. Meyer
81 Stefano Micozzi
82 Robin Moyer
83 Seny Norasingh
84 Antonello Nusca
85 Randy Olson
86 Graeme Outerbridge
87 Daniele Pellegrini
88 Fabrizio Pesce
89 Giovanna Piemonti
90 Bill Pierce
91 Vittoriano Rastelli
92 Jim Richardson
93 Rick Rickman
94 Joe Rossi
95 Enrico Sacchetti
96 George Steinmetz
97 Patrick Tehan
98 David C. Turnley
99 Peter Turnley
100 Jerry Valente
101 Mauro Vallinotto
102 Sandro Vermini
103 Mark S. Wexler
104 Michael S. Yamashita
105 Franco Zecchin

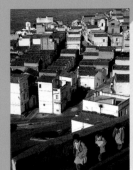

Gianni Berengo Gardin, Potenza

Graeme Outerbridge, Val Gardena

Barry Lewis, Milan

Gianni Giansanti, Alicudi

Torin Boyd, Corleone

• Bressanone/93
• Val Gardena/86
TRENTINO-
ALTO ADIGE
• Domodossola/9
• Cortina d'Ampezzo/19

• Courmayeur/5
VALLE
D'AOSTA
FRIULI-
VENEZIA
GIULIA
• Udine/43

• Como/28

• Asolo/52
• Brescia/77
• Treviso/48
• Milan/33, 37, 38, 49, 53, 62, 64, 71, 90
• Vicenza/32
• Vercelli/13   LOMBARDY
• Verona/36
• Trieste/34, 46
• Turin/67, 103
VENETO
• Venice/54, 80

PIEDMONT

LIGURIA
• Parma/75
• Genoa/58, 102
• Modena/96
• Portofino/17
• Bologna/79, 82
• Ravenna/85
• Alassio/91
EMILIA-ROMAGNA
• San Remo/51
• Manarola/94
• Rimini/68
• Pietrasanta/20
• Lucca/76
• Florence/10, 29, 41
• Greve/61
MARCHE
• Siena/24
• Ancona/59
• Monte Oliveto Maggiore/25
TUSCANY
• Perugia/35
• Porto San Giorgio/97
UMBRIA
• Assisi/27
• Orvieto/3
• Alberese/30
• Spoleto/50
• Viterbo/78
• Gran Sasso/87
ABRUZZO
• Bracciano/70
• Ovindoli/2
• Sulmona/73
• Rome/4, 21, 22, 26, 31, 40, 42, 55, 60, 74, 81, 84, 89, 95
• Nemi/39
• Agnone/56
LAZIO
• San Giovanni Rotondo/83
• La Maddalena/63
• San Biagio Saracinisco/100
• Nettuno/72
MOLISE
• Campobasso/101
• Fondi/65
• Gaeta/11
CAMPANIA
PUGLIA
• Bari/14
• Naples/1, 6, 7
• Nuoro/45
• Positano/104
• Potenza/12
• Martina Franca/16
SARDINIA
• Matera/66
• Taranto/105
BASILICATA
• Cagliari/99
• Lecce/92

CALABRIA

• Lamezia Terme/57

• Alicudi/47
• Locri/23
• Palermo/98
• Reggio di Calabria/44
• Corleone/15
• Mazara del Vallo/8
SICILY
• Agrigento/18
• Catania/69

• Noto/88

Eddie Adams, Naples

John Marmaras, Rimini

Ricardo DeAratanha, Assisi

P. F. Bentley, Gaeta

211

1. Eric Lars Bakke

2. Eric Lars Bakke

1. Team Roma: The shoot over, staffers recline on the steps of the church of Santa Maria Maggiore in Rome. Front row: Arnaldo Rovinelli, Blake Hallanan, Leah Painter Roberts, Linda Lamb. Middle: Nadia Bernardi, Massimo Comito, Mimi Murphy, Bruna Colarossi. Back: Karen Bakke, Bill Messing, Patti Richards, Claire Schiffman.
2. Italian 101: Project Director Roy Rowan translates Assignment Editor Massimo Comito's work into English.
3. Time out: Leah Painter Roberts, Patti Richards, Karen Bakke, and Jennifer Erwitt in a rare moment of relaxation.

3. Linda Lamb

4. Eric Lars Bakke

4. Sponsorship Director Cathy Qualy stocks up on film kits.
5. Rocking out: Karen Bakke and Linda Lamb share a piece of the shoreline on Capri.

5. Doug Howell

"It's going to rain," said Grazia Neri. It was February, and

Italy lay in the throes of a protracted drought, with no end in sight. The ski season had ended before it began, and water rationing had been instituted in Milan. But now, upon hearing the news that 100 of the world's great photographers would soon be fanning out across the land, she knew the drought would end. Neri, a photographers' representative regarded by many in the Italian photo community as Mother Superior, knows a thing or two about taking pictures. And her logic was infallible: Anytime you assemble that many photographers in one place, all praying for perfect weather, chances are it's going to pour. She didn't know whether to laugh or cry.

Cut to April. For three months, first at their headquarters in San Francisco and now in Rome, project logistics director Jennifer Erwitt, managing editor Bill Messing, and the rest of the *Day in the Life* crew had been researching and organizing to the point of obsession in preparation for April 27, the day of the shoot. As they rushed around a fresco-bedecked office crammed with Macintosh computers, telephones, fax machines, and discarded pizza wrappers, Erwitt and Messing paused from time to time to gaze out the window at the torrents of water cascading down onto Rome's Via Cavour. Despite all their other worries, they were really only wondering about one thing: Would this *maledetta pioggia*, this cursed rain, so casually predicted by Grazia Neri months earlier, ever stop?

It had better.

From the choice of the day itself down to the last train connection, no detail had been overlooked. Erwitt and company—office manager Linda Lamb, production coordinator Kate Yuschenkoff, and production assistant Arnaldo Rovinelli—had created and fine-tuned complex schedules for the whirlwind week the photographers would spend in Italy. Publicity director Patti Richards and assistants Claire Schiffman and Jacaranda Falck had talked to countless television, print, and radio reporters in an effort to see that every one of Italy's 60 million people knew of the project. And travel director Karen Bakke, charged with the unenviable task of getting the photographers into Rome from around the world, then to and from their destinations within Italy, and finally back home again, had been burning up the phone and fax lines for weeks.

Sponsorship director Cathy Qualy and manager Blake Hallanan had spent the time recruiting corporate sponsors to help underwrite the project's huge operating costs. Ray DeMoulin, president of Eastman Kodak's Professional Photography Division, was the first to come on board. In addition to providing thousands of rolls of film, Kodak would sponsor a photography workshop for Roman schoolchildren, wine and dine the photographers at an elaborate banquet, and even set up a telephone hotline to answer any technical questions that might arise on location.

Jeff Kriendler at Pan Am signed up the airline for its third *Day in the Life* project with a promise of over a hundred round-trip tickets. Kimio Shioiri at Nikon supplied cameras and offered to send two top technicians—Susumu Kataoka from Tokyo and Danilo Cinel from Konos in Florence—to set up a free camera clinic in Rome, ultimately servicing over 250 instruments in 30 hours. More support came from Bettoja Hotels, Avis Autonoleggio, and Credito Italiano. Apple Computer even loaned computers.

Now, on April 20, the pulse in the Rome office was quickening. The talent on whose shoulders the success of the book would ultimately rest, the photographers, were due to arrive in two days. Along with artistic flair and dedicated professionalism, they were sure to bring with them a new set of complications. Could they also, one dared to hope, bring along some sunshine?

As Erwitt and Messing turned their attention back to the business of finalizing photo assignments and triple-checking hotel arrangements, they reminded themselves that the weather is one of the variables that make the *Day in the Life* books—of which Italy is the tenth—so special. The rules are simple: All the photos that appear in the book must be taken between 12:01 AM and 12:00 midnight on a single day. Whatever the weather, the shutters of the 100 photographers, including 23 Italian *fotoreporters* and six Pulitzer Prize winners, would open and close countless times. Erwitt, a veteran of nine *Day in the Life* projects, consoled herself with the knowledge that these were, after all, the world's best photojournalists, accustomed to making great photographs in conditions far more treacherous than a spring rainstorm.

The one-day, come-what-may format gave *A Day in the Life of Italy* some common ground with its predecessors—Australia, Hawaii, Canada, Japan, America, the Soviet Union, Spain, California, and China. But this would also be a *Day in the Life* book unlike any other, because Italy, as painters, poets, gourmands, sun-worshipers, and every other kind of sensualist has always known, is a place of rare appeal. Clearly, it would make a delicious choice of venue for the 1990 *Day in the Life* book, albeit a challenging one for photographers and project organizers—for how do you take fresh and fascinating pictures of a country that is among the most visited and photographed places on earth?

To begin with, you find the right people to dream up shooting assignments—people who know the difference between a story and a stereotype, a character and a cliché. They would have to offer intimate first-hand knowledge not just of Italy's geography and history, but of her values and ideas as well.

They came from all over. Leah Painter Roberts, formerly a student in Bologna, took leave from her post as a senior film reviewer at *National Geographic*. Mimi Murphy and Ann Wise took time out from their assigning duties at Time-Life's Rome bureau. Veteran newspaper journalist Massimo Comito brought knowledge of the south from stints as a reporter in Naples and Palermo. Nadia Bernardi offered a background in travel. And for editorial director Roy Rowan, a 40-year veteran at Time-Life, the project was a homecoming of sorts—he had been Rome bureau chief in the 1950s. Together, their efforts would guarantee that *A Day in the Life of Italy* would eschew the obvious in documenting the diverse, enchanting, and at times infuriating land that is modern Italy.

On April 22, the photographers arrived. The news that greeted them, many of whom had left assignments in such hot spots as Berlin, Beirut, Lithuania, and El Salvador for this shoot, did not bode well. In *Corriere della Sera*, one of Italy's top dailies, the lead story was headlined "Train and Plane Strikes to Begin Tomorrow" and began, "This will be a tough week for anyone who has to travel." Anyone, say, like a world-class photographer on a tight deadline.

In the space of a few weeks, staffers had already cheerfully endured strikes by telephone operators, taxi drivers, even chambermaids. But the prospect of widespread transportation stoppages at a time like this seemed cruel indeed. A look inside the newspapers offered some solace, with major features touting the arrival of the photographers and explaining the idea behind the shoot. Dozens more articles were to follow. But none of that would matter if all the photographers were stuck in Rome. Suddenly the rain didn't seem like such a big deal. "Let it rain if it has to," the DITLI staff was thinking. "Just so long as the trains keep running..."

6. Ethan Hoffman

7. Patrick Tehan

8. Paul Chesley

9. Cathy Quealy

10. Linda Lamb

6. Presidential summit: Italian President Francesco Cossiga greets Collins president Bruce Gray at the Quirinale.
7. At ease: Michele McNally and Susan Vermazen find a very safe location in Italy's presidential palace.
8. Junior achievement: Photographer/editor duo Joe and Michele McNally attend Kodak's photography workshop for children with their daughter Caitlin.
9. Fab four: Photographers George Steinmetz, Paul Chesley, Mark Wexler, and Claus Meyer set out for parts unknown.
10. Family ties: Project Director Jennifer Erwitt with her photographer father Elliott.

11. Linda Lamb

12. Jean-Pierre Laffont

The rain finally lifted–or so it seemed–on April 23. Gathered at the Bettoja Hotel for a briefing session, the photographers learned for the first time where they would go and what they would shoot. The room fell silent as they pored over their assignments, trying to visualize their one-day whirlwind. The office crew passed out kits containing film, T-shirts, caption books, and cameras, and informally shared secrets of surviving in Italy, including advice on how to get in and out of a restaurant fast. "We were the first people ever to come to Rome and go hungry," said Bill Messing. "It was taking us three hours to get a meal, and we just didn't have the time. Later we learned how to grease the wheels a bit and speed things up."

The afternoon was dedicated to the Kodak Children's Workshop at Villa Borghese Park, where the photographers were to hand out cameras and give lessons on the spot to 100 Roman children. The kids got there first while the photographers sat in Rome's notorious traffic; it fell to Kodak's Giorgio Facchinetti to placate the restive tribe during the interim, a feat carried off with characteristic artistry. The work of some of these young *paparazzi* appears on pages 126 and 127.

The official group portrait followed, taken by Doug Menuez in front of the Campidoglio, the capitol square designed by Michelangelo. And as the sun set, staff and photographers were whisked off to the Villa Miani for the first in a run of parties hosted by *Day in the Life of Italy* sponsors–this one by Nikon. It was a first day that reminded *Day in the Life* veterans why they come back year after year, and convinced newcomers to ask for a spot on the next year's project. Said first-timer Ernesto Bazan: "Spending time with the other photographers is one of the best things about the project. The sense of camaraderie is exhilarating."

On Tuesday came a private audience with Italy's president, Francesco Cossiga, although there were some anxious moments when Cossiga's guards informed Collins' president Bruce Gray that no photographs could be permitted in the presidential *palazzo*. With some timely assistance from Kodak's Luigi Negrini, Gray finally convinced the princes of protocol that any self-respecting photographer would sooner give up his clothes than his camera. The doors swung open on the spot, and the grateful photographers took advantage of the occasion to present President Cossiga with a complete set of *Day in the Life* books and a 1918-vintage Kodak camera.

11. Man on the move: Ricardo DeAratanha checks out of the Bettoja Hotel en route to his assignment in Assisi.
12. Rome or Bust: Jean-Pierre Laffont looks for souvenirs in the prop department at Cinecittà.
13. Say *formaggio*: Doug Menuez prepares to shoot the group portrait on the steps of Rome's Campidoglio.

13. Franco Zecchin

Hours of individual assignment briefings were to follow, the day only drawing to a close with a lavish banquet, courtesy of Kodak, in the storybook ballrooms of the Palazzo del Drago. Back at headquarters, the staff fretted; the rains still threatened, the train strike had begun, and the photographers were due to leave for their assignments the very next day.

On Wednesday, fate intervened; since it was a national holiday, the forty-fifth anniversary of Italy's liberation from German troops, the train strike was postponed for a day–the theory being that no one would be traveling anyway. Avis' provision of some 70 automobiles, along with an offer to keep offices open as late as necessary despite the holiday, gave extra assurance that no photographer would be stranded.

Safely ensconced at their shooting locations, the photographers spent the next day scouting and making last-minute arrangements. For many of them, the hardest part of the research day was trying to slow down the creative juices long enough to steal some rest. Most of them would be up at midnight to begin shooting; to begin freezing in time this ordinary day in a most extraordinary country.

As they rose early on April 27, the photographers found a cloudless night sky sparkling with stars. And when the sun dawned over the Adriatic Sea a few hours later, the staff on Rome's Via Cavour put away their umbrellas. Shoot day was clear and warm.

Per forza, Italy-watchers will say; of course. Italians have always adored putting on *la bella figura*–a good show, your best face. And what kind of figure would Italy have cut by inviting 100 of the world's best photographers for a day, and then soaking them in rain? The rains leading up to the shoot day were a tease, in the best theatrical tradition of a theatrical country.

14. Steve Tello

14. Double take: Peripatetic twin photographers Peter and David Turnley check out the view from the other side of the camera for an ABC-TV documentary.
15. Model citizens: Photographer Dana Fineman encourages her subjects to do what comes naturally.

15. Jeff Kriendler

In a feat of impeccable timing, the train strike, like the rain, was magically erased on April 27. Saturday the photographers began returning to Rome little the worse for wear. At a final soirée in the dramatic confines of the wine cellar at the Bettoja Hotel, they began trading stories of their forays into all corners of the place that Italians call *il Bel Paese*, the beautiful country.

Several had been accompanied by video crews from ABC, CBS, and the Italian state network, RAI. Edoardo Fornaciari had been assigned to spend the morning in a police helicopter, photographing Rome's notorious morning rush hour. But because of a snafu with insurance papers, the chopper's takeoff was delayed, and Fornaciari didn't get airborne until 9:30–far too late to capture the torture trail of Fiats and Alfas winding their way into the Eternal City. No matter: A police officer in the helicopter simply radioed down to his colleagues on the ground, who proceeded to roadblock several streets and create an artificial traffic jam for the camera. Fornaciari politely declined to photograph the staged event.

In San Remo, on the Riviera of Flowers on Italy's northwest coast, photographer Judy Griesedieck's interpreter struggled to navigate the cobblestone streets and steep steps in a pair of high heels. When Griesedieck gently suggested that the interpreter might want to change shoes, she dutifully disappeared for several minutes–returning, in the spirit of *la bella figura*, with even higher heels.

And Richard Marshall of the *St. Paul Pioneer Press Dispatch*, one of a handful of Italian-American photographers to visit his family's ancestral village, stood in front of his mother's house in Santa Maria di Licodia, a Sicilian village at the base of Mt. Etna. "My mother left when she was ten years old," he said. "But she always described the house and garden to me in detail. And it was exactly as she said. I broke down and cried. I called her on the phone and she couldn't talk because she was crying. I paid $20 for us to cry over the phone." Marshall spent much of the day photographing his second and third cousins, whom he had never met. "The biggest problem I had," he said, "was getting away from the table after lunch to go shoot in the town. They didn't want to let me go."

Although April 29 was departure day, Italy had a similar pull on many other photographers. Jerry Valente, another Italian-American photographer who visited his family, said, "I'm not looking forward to going back to New York. After being in Italy, I pity New Yorkers." Added David Turnley, Paris-based photographer for the *Detroit Free Press* and a 1990 Pulitzer Prize winner, "The light in Italy is extremely sensual. I had a lovely time; it seems like the right way to live in so many respects. I felt fortunate just to be able to spend a day in Italy."

All told, that one day in Italy was to consume 3,318 rolls of film–119,448 individual slides–which were logged on the spot and rushed back to the United States. Pan Am's Kriendler went so far as to provide seats for that precious cargo, so that it might never escape Jennifer Erwitt's watchful eye. Extraordinary provisions in both Rome and New York guaranteed that the film would also escape the scourge of every photographer, the airport x-ray.

Within days processing was complete, and in no time ten top picture editors–newly arrived from points as far-flung as New York, Barcelona, and Milan–descended on the catch. Their eagerness to seek out each precious needle in this particular haystack was tempered only by the knowledge that but a week remained to narrow the field to a mere 300 frames. From there it would fall to art director Jennifer Barry to give *A Day in the Life of Italy*–better known in Italy as *Un giorno nella vita dell'Italia*, published by Rizzoli–its final shape.

This book, the end result, is Italy's ultimate *bella figura*, a collective, one-day vision of a magical place. How else but magic to explain the rains stopping and the trains starting? Or the magnetic lure of the Colosseum? Or a country surviving, indeed thriving, despite having had more than 40 different governments since the end of World War II?

This is Italy's genius, this magic born of blurring the line between the real and the phantasmagorical. "If you didn't know better, you'd think you were on a movie set," said Bill Messing. "We all kept fighting the urge to go around behind things to see if they were real." For one day in April, 1990, 100 of the world's best photographers went behind the scenes, looking to create a little magic of their own–trying to see what is real and what is not and, like the Italians themselves, shrugging it off when they couldn't tell the difference.

16. Mike Davis

16. It's not just a job, it's an adventure: P.F. Bentley regales Managing Editor Bill Messing with stories of his shoot at the NATO base in Gaeta.
17. Picture editors are accustomed to handling fragile slides with great delicacy. Left to right: Amilcare Ponchielli, Sandra Eisert, Michele McNally, Susan Vermazen, Peter Howe, Guy Cooper, Michele Stephenson, Maddy Miller, Alfonso Gutiérrez Escera, Mike Davis.

17. P.F. Bentley

18. P.F. Bentley

18. Floor show: Art Director Jenny Barry and assistant Kari Ontko lay out the book.
19. The Collins staff reunites in San Francisco after the shoot.

19. P.F. Bentley

Photographers' Biographies

Eddie Adams
American/New York, New York
With a Pulitzer Prize, three George Polk Memorial Awards, a World Press Grand Award, and six New York Press Photographer of the Year Awards to his credit, Adams is one of the most decorated and published photographers in the United States. He has photographed leaders in all fields, from heads of state to superstars of film, sports, and high fashion. He is founder and director of the Eddie Adams Workshop, a yearly event designed to promote development of talented new photographers.

Monica Almeida   Vietnam 1989

Monica Almeida
American/New York, New York
Almeida began her career at the *Los Angeles Times*, where she was part of the team of journalists awarded the 1984 Pulitzer Prize for coverage of California's Hispanic community. Since 1986 she has been a staff photographer for the *New York Daily News*, covering a variety of news and feature stories.

Lexine M. Alpert
American/Berkeley, California
In 1988 Alpert left behind a ten-year career as a medical social worker to embark on a new one as a photojournalist. She won first place in the 1989 Greg Robinson Photojournalism Awards at San Francisco State University, as well as first place in the 1989 documentary photography category at the San Francisco Art Academy. Italy is her first *Day in the Life* book.

Eric Lars Bakke
American/Denver, Colorado
Formerly the chief photographer for the *Denver Post*, Bakke is now a member of the Picture Group photo agency and a contributor to Allsport USA. During his seventeen-year career he has covered events ranging from the World Series and the Super Bowl to insect infestation in Utah and fire storms in Yellowstone National Park. His work has been published in an array of magazines including *Time*, *Sports Illustrated*, *Business Week*, and *National Geographic*. In 1985 he received honorable mention in the National Press Photographers Association Pictures of the Year competition.

Bruno Barbey
French/Paris
Barbey became a professional photographer after studying at the École des Arts et Métiers in Vevey, Switzerland, and became a full member of the Magnum photo agency in 1968. His work has been featured in dozens of books and periodicals. He was awarded the French National Order of Merit in 1985.

Letizia Battaglia   Palermo 1986

Letizia Battaglia
Italian/Palermo
Battaglia is the publisher of *Grandevù*, a monthly magazine of photography, politics, and culture. She also serves as co-editor at La Luna, a publishing house that features primarily works by women. In 1985 she won the prestigious W. Eugene Smith Award for her work on the Mafia. Since 1986, she has held a number of positions in Palermo's municipal government as a representative of the Green Party.

Ernesto Bazan
Italian/New York, New York
Bazan's book *The Perpetual Past* documents the Italian-American community in New York City. He was named Young Photographer of the Year in Arles, France in 1982, and won first prize in the news photo category in Arles the following year. Italy is his first *Day in the Life* book.

Nicole Bengiveno   Moscow 1989

Nicole Bengiveno
American/New York, New York
Bengiveno joined the staff of the *New York Daily News* in 1986 after eight years with the *San Francisco Examiner*. She was named Bay Area Press Photographer of the Year in 1979. In 1985 she was a finalist for the W. Eugene Smith Award for her work on the AIDS epidemic, and in 1987 and 1989 she won first-place honors in feature photography from the New York Associated Press for her work from the Soviet Union.

P.F. Bentley
American/Stinson Beach, California
Bentley is a *Time* magazine photographer whose assignments have taken him to Central America, where he has covered elections in both El Salvador and Panama. His awards include first-place honors in the National Press Photographers Association Pictures of the Year competition in 1984 and 1988 for his coverage of the U.S. presidential campaigns. Italy is his eighth *Day in the Life* book.

Gianni Berengo Gardin
Italian/Milan
The creator of some 150 photography books on Italy and Europe, Berengo Gardin became a professional photographer in 1962 at the age of 32. He lived in Rome, Paris, Venice, and Switzerland before settling in Milan.

Marcello Bertinetti
Italian/Vercelli
Bertinetti's career as a professional photographer began with a 1978 trip from Italy to Nepal by van. His work has since been published in most leading magazines. He has also produced a series of books about the world's great cities, published by Italy's Edizione White Star—the most successful of which, *New York*, has sold more than 400,000 copies.

Enrico Bossan
Italian/Padua
A professional photographer since 1984, Bossan has exhibited his work at several international shows, including the Houston FotoFest (1986), Amsterdam Foto (1986), and the Freiburg International Photography Exposition (1988). His photography is included in the collection of the Bibliothèque Nationale de Paris.

Torin Boyd
American/Tokyo
A veteran of several *Day in the Life* projects, Boyd began his career as a surfing photographer at the age of 17 in Cocoa Beach, Florida. He is now based in Tokyo, and his work appears in *Fortune*, *Newsweek*, *Time*, *U.S. News & World Report*, and several Japanese magazines. He recently published his first calendar on Japan through Landmark Publishing.

Marilyn Bridges   Wiltshire 1985

Marilyn Bridges
American/New York, New York
An accomplished pilot of both single- and multi-engine aircraft, Bridges is the author of *Markings: Aerial Views of Sacred Landscapes*, published by Aperture. Her photographs are part of numerous public collections, including New York's Museum of Modern Art, the International Center of Photography, the George Eastman House, the Bibliothèque Nationale de Paris, and the Canadian Centre for Architecture. A 1981 graduate of the Rochester Institute of Technology, she has since been awarded a Guggenheim Fellowship, a Fulbright-grant, and a National Endowment for the Arts grant.

Michael Bryant
American/Philadelphia, Pennsylvania
A staff photographer at the *Philadelphia Inquirer*, Bryant was named Pennsylvania Photographer of the Year in 1988. He worked for the *San Jose Mercury News* from 1980 to 1986, during which time he was named Photographer of the Year in both California and Michigan.

René Burri
Swiss/Zürich

Burri's work has been featured in dozens of books and exhibitions since he began traveling the world as a photographer in 1955. A major retrospective of his work, *René Burri One World*, was presented in 1984 at the Kunsthaus Zürich and the Palais de Tokyo in Paris.

Bill Cafer Jr.   Washington, D.C. 1986

Bill Cafer Jr.
American/Rochester, New York

A graduate of the Rochester Institute of Technology, Cafer is currently a staff photographer with the Eastman Kodak Company. His work has appeared in the Grand Central and Times Square displays in New York City, as well as in annual reports, television commercials, and advertising for Kodak.

Romano Cagnoni
Italian/Pietrasanta

Called by former London *Sunday Times* editor Harold Evans "one of the five most famous photographers in the world," Cagnoni spent 26 years living and working in London. He was the first photographer to document the starvation in Biafra, and his work has been published in dozens of magazines and books.

Elisabetta Catalano
Italian/Rome

Catalano's portraits appear regularly in Italian publications, and she has also been published in both the U.S. and French editions of *Vogue*. Her work has been the focus of shows in Rome, Milan, Venice, Florence, Boston, and Paris.

Paul Chesley
American/Aspen, Colorado

As a freelance photographer with the National Geographic Society since 1975, Chesley has traveled regularly to Europe and Asia. Solo exhibitions of his work have appeared in museums in London, Tokyo, and New York. Italy is the ninth *Day in the Life* project for Chesley, who is also a frequent contributor to *Life*, *Connoisseur*, *Fortune*, *Time*, *GEO*, and *Stern*.

Francesco Paolo Cito
Italian/Milan

A native of Naples, Cito was among the first photographers to enter Afghanistan clandestinely after the Soviet invasion in 1979; ten years later, he returned to document the effects of the Soviet withdrawal. He has been to Lebanon on assignment seven times, and during the past three years he has made several trips to the Occupied Territories. His work has been published in *Life*, *Stern*, *Paris Match*, *Epoca*, *Europeo*, and other leading magazines.

Bradley E. Clift
American/Hartford, Connecticut

A graduate of the University of Minnesota School of Journalism, Clift is now a staff photographer for the *Hartford Courant*. He is the recipient of more than 100 local, state, and regional photography awards. In 1986 he won the National Press Photographers Association Photographer of the Year award and a World Press Photo Foundation award; in 1987 he won the Robert F. Kennedy Award for Photojournalism. The cover of *A Day in the Life of California* features one of his works.

Pedro Coll
Spanish/Mallorca

Coll has traveled on assignment to five continents since becoming a professional photographer in 1975. He works for photo agencies in England, West Germany, Spain, Italy, Japan, Australia, and the United States. He is currently at work on three book projects.

Ricardo DeAratanha   San Francisco 1988

Ricardo DeAratanha
Brazilian/Los Angeles

Currently a staff photographer for the *Los Angeles Times*, DeAratanha began his career with *Jornal do Brasil*. His work has appeared in numerous American and Brazilian publications, and he is a three-time award winner in the Nikon International Photo Contest.

Mario De Biasi
Italian/Milan

De Biasi had his first one-man show in 1948. Five years later he joined the staff of *Epoca*, for which he produced hundreds of covers and thousands of photographs from around the world. More than twenty books of his photographs have been published in Italy.

Guglielmo de' Micheli
Italian/Florence

De' Micheli began publishing his photography in 1979 at the age of 17. His work has appeared in *Sports Illustrated*, *Life*, the *New York Times Magazine*, and other publications.

Jay Dickman   China 1989

Jay Dickman
American/Denver, Colorado

A 1983 Pulitzer Prize winner and gold medalist in the World Press Photo Foundation competition, Dickman was a newspaper photographer in Dallas for 16 years before moving to Denver to devote himself full-time to a career as a freelancer. He recently completed a ten-week assignment in Papua New Guinea for *National Geographic*. His work appears in *Time*, *Life*, *GEO*, *Bunte*, and *Stern*, and has been honored by Sigma Delta Chi, the Society of Professional Journalists. He has participated in all ten *Day in the Life* projects.

Don Doll, S.J.
American/Omaha, Nebraska

A professor of fine arts and photography at Creighton University in Omaha, Doll recently completed an eight-month study of the Athapaskan Indians along the Yukon River in Alaska that appeared in *National Geographic*. In the 1989 Pictures of the Year competition, sponsored by the National Press Photographers Association, he won first place in the magazine feature photograph category.

John Dominis
American/New York, New York

In his 22 years on staff at *Life* magazine, Dominis covered such major events as the Korean War, President Kennedy's visit to Berlin, and Woodstock. He is a former picture editor of both *People* and *Sports Illustrated*, and in 1966 he was named Magazine Photographer of the Year by the University of Missouri.

Elliott Erwitt | Personal Exposures

Elliott Erwitt   1989

Elliott Erwitt
American/New York, New York

Erwitt was born in Paris and grew up in Milan before moving to the United States at age 11 in 1939. He has had one-man shows in museums and galleries around the world, including New York's Museum of Modern Art, the Smithsonian Institution, the Chicago Art Institute, and the Kunsthaus Zürich. A large retrospective exhibition of his work was held in Paris, Cologne, and Tokyo in the fall of 1988 to accompany publication of his book *Elliott Erwitt/Personal Exposures* by W.W. Norton.

Misha Erwitt
American/New York, New York

A native New Yorker, Erwitt has been taking pictures since he was 11 years old, and is on staff at the *New York Daily News*. His work has been published in *American Photographer*, *Esquire*, *People*, *USA Today*, and *Manhattan, inc.*, and he has participated in seven *Day in the Life* projects. He is affiliated with the Magnum photo agency and is the son of fellow *Day in the Life* photographer Elliott Erwitt.

Richard Eskite
American/San Francisco, California

Eskite is best known for his corporate and advertising still-life photography. He has received awards from Printing Industries of America, Inc., Consolidated Paper Companies, Inc., and the San Francisco Art Directors Club. His clients include Apple Computer, Del Monte Foods, Ghirardelli Chocolate, Levi Strauss, and the Raychem Corporation.

Melissa Farlow
American/Pittsburgh, Pennsylvania

In 1975 Farlow was a member of the *Louisville Courier-Journal* and *Louisville Times* photography staff that received a Pulitzer Prize for its coverage of desegregation of the public schools. Now a staff photographer for the *Pittsburgh Press*, she was named Pennsylvania Photographer of the Year in 1988; she is also a two-time Greater Pittsburgh Photographer of the Year.

Dana Fineman
American/New York, New York

A member of the Sygma photo agency, Fineman studied at the Art Center College of Design in Pasadena. Her work appears regularly in *New York Magazine*, *People*, *Time*, *Newsweek*, and *Stern*. In May of 1986, following shoot day for *A Day in the Life of America*, she married photographer Gerd Ludwig, with 200 of the world's best photojournalists covering the wedding.

Franco Fontana   Phoenix 1989

Franco Fontana
Italian/Modena

Fontana first exhibited his work in his native Modena in 1968, and since then he has published work around the world. His photography is included in the permanent collections of more than 60 museums.

Edoardo Fornaciari
Italian/Rome

Fornaciari worked as a fashion photographer in Milan until 1979, when he came to Rome to establish a career as a freelancer. He is a native of Parma.

Dino Fracchia   Modena 1990

Dino Fracchia

Italian/Milan

Over the past two decades Fracchia has covered many of Italy's most important stories, including the 1976 earthquake in the country's northeast, the dioxin leak near Milan the same year, and NATO maneuvers and the growth of the peace movement. His work has been published in *Newsweek*, the *New York Times*, *Epoca*, *L'Espresso*, and *Europeo*.

Rudi Frey

Austrian/Rome

As a *Time* contract photographer since 1978, Frey has covered the kidnapping and murder of Italian politician Aldo Moro, the growth of Solidarity in Poland, and the Israeli invasion of Lebanon, among other major stories. He won the 1981 Robert Capa Gold Medal Citation from the Overseas Press Club for his coverage of Poland.

J.W. Fry   Texas 1989

J.W. Fry

American/Rochester, New York

After receiving his degree in photography from East Texas State University, Fry worked as a freelance photographer in Dallas. In 1989 he was accepted to the Eddie Adams Workshop, where he won a one-year fellowship with the Professional Photography Division of the Eastman Kodak Company.

Raphaël Gaillarde

French/Paris

Gaillarde is one of the leading news photographers of Gamma Presse Images. His pictures of world events have appeared in many European magazines, including *GEO*, and he has participated in several *Day in the Life* projects.

Sam Garcia

American/New York, New York

Formerly an Atlanta-based freelance photographer, Garcia is now on staff with Nikon Professional Services. In his 14 years with Nikon he has covered most major sporting events, including four Olympic Games, and he has trained America's space shuttle astronauts to use 35mm still equipment. Italy is the seventh *Day in the Life* project for Garcia, who is also on the faculty of the Eddie Adams Workshop.

Georg Gerster

Swiss/Zürich

Gerster has freelanced as a writer and photographer since receiving his Ph.D. in German literature from the University of Zürich in 1956. He is a frequent contributor to *Neue Zürcher Zeitung*, *National Geographic* and *GEO*. His work has also been published in the London *Sunday Times Magazine*, *Paris Match*, *Epoca*, and *Omni*, and by Time-Life Books.

Gianni Giansanti

Italian/Rome

Giansanti has traveled to Lebanon, Poland, El Salvador, Haiti, Peru, the United States, and Iceland for the Sygma photo agency. He won first prize in the 1988 World Press Photo Foundation awards for his coverage of the Pope.

Diego Goldberg

Argentine/Buenos Aires

After beginning his photographic career in Latin America as a correspondent for *Camera Press*, Goldberg moved to Paris in 1977 as a Sygma staff photographer. In 1980 he moved to New York, only returning to his native Argentina in 1985. His work has been featured in the world's major magazines, and in 1984 he won a World Press Photo Foundation award.

Lynn Goldsmith

American/New York, New York

Goldsmith's work has appeared on the covers of *Life*, *Newsweek*, *Elle*, *Rolling Stone*, and *People* magazines. Among her honors are awards from the World Press Photo Foundation, the Nikon International Photo Contest, and the Arles Rencontres. She is the founder of the LGI photo agency, which specializes in contemporary celebrity portraiture.

Bill Greene

American/Boston, Massachusetts

Greene was named New England Photographer of the Year four times in a row while at the *Patriot Ledger* in Quincy, Massachusetts. He has won Photographer of the Year honors from the Boston Press Photographers Association five times, and in 1987 was named Photographer of the Year by the National Press Photographers Association. He is currently a staff photographer for the *Boston Globe*.

Judy Griesedieck

American/Minneapolis, Minnesota

During six years as a staff photographer for the *San Jose Mercury News*, Griesedieck covered such events as the 1984 Democratic National Convention, the Calgary Winter Olympics, and the Super Bowl. She was California Photographer of the Year in 1986, and in 1987 was the runner-up in the Canon Photo Essayist category in the University of Missouri Pictures of the Year contest. Previously she was a staff photographer for the *Hartford Courant*, where she was named Connecticut Photographer of the Year in 1983. She recently relocated to Minneapolis to start a freelance photography business.

Annie Griffiths Belt

American/Washington, D.C.

After graduating from the University of Minnesota with a degree in photojournalism, Griffiths Belt began her career with the *Worthington Daily Globe* in southern Minnesota. In 1978 she began assignment work for *National Geographic* and has since worked on more than two dozen magazine and book projects. Her work has also appeared in *Smithsonian*, *Newsweek*, *GEO*, *National Wildlife*, *Merian*, and *Stern*, and she has exhibited in New York, Washington, D.C., Moscow, and Tokyo. She has received awards from the National Press Photographers Association, the Associated Press, the National Organization for Women, and the White House News Photographers Association.

Volker Hinz

German/New York, New York

For the last 16 years Hinz has been a staff photographer for *Stern* magazine. His pictures also appear in many other news and feature magazines including *Vanity Fair*, *Time*, *Newsweek*, *New York Magazine*, *Life*, *Paris Match*, and *GEO*.

Ethan Hoffman

American/New York, New York

A photographer and editor who divided his time between New York and Tokyo, Hoffman published his work in *Life*, the *New York Times Magazine*, *Stern*, *GEO*, *Fortune*, and other major magazines. His first book, *Concrete Mama: Prison Profiles from Walla Walla*, was nominated for the National Book Award in 1981. His last book was *Butoh: Dance of the Dark Soul*, published by Aperture. He was director of the Picture Project, a not-for-profit publisher specializing in photography books. He died on June 1, 1990 following an accidental fall while on assignment. He was 40 years old.

Mark Kauffman Rhode Island 1952

Mark Kauffman

American/San Luis Obispo, California

Kauffman was the founding photographer of *Sports Illustrated* and shot the covers for the magazine's first two issues in 1954. He worked for *Life* magazine for 30 years, and he was the first magazine photographer ever to win the coveted Grand Award from the White House News Photographers. He is now a full-time lecturer at California Polytechnic State University.

Nick Kelsh   China 1989

Nick Kelsh

American/Philadelphia, Pennsylvania

A native of North Dakota, Kelsh has produced award-winning photos for *Time*, *Life*, *Newsweek*, *National Geographic*, *Forbes*, *Fortune*, and *BusinessWeek*. In 1986 he left the *Philadelphia Inquirer* to co-found Kelsh Marr Studios, a company that specializes in design and photography for annual reports and other corporate publications. Kelsh pictures are featured on the covers both of *A Day in the Life of China* and of *The Power to Heal*, published by Prentice Hall Press.

Robb Kendrick

American/Houston, Texas

Kendrick began his freelance photography career in 1986. Since then he has published work in *Time*, *Life*, *Sports Illustrated*, *National Geographic*, *GEO*, *Merian*, *Fortune*, and the *New York Times*. A recent solo exhibition at the FotoFest in Houston featured his work on Texas ranching.

Roberto Koch   Moscow 1988

Roberto Koch

Italian/Rome

Koch contributes regularly to *Epoca*, *Stern*, *The Independent*, *Time*, *Fortune*, *Vanity Fair*, the *New York Times*, and *Europeo*. He is a founding member of Agenzia Contrasto, one of Italy's leading photo agencies, and has exhibited his work in Arles, Brussels, Cologne, Athens, Prague, Paris, Houston, and several Italian cities.

Steve Krongard

American/New York, New York
One of the country's busiest advertising and corporate photographers, Krongard counts Amtrak, Qantas, and Bell South among his recent clients. He is on the faculty of the School of Visual Arts in New York City. Italy is his eighth *Day in the Life* project.

Jean-Pierre Laffont

French/New York, New York
Laffont attended the prestigious School of Graphic Arts in Vevey, Switzerland and later became a founding member of both Gamma and Sygma photo agencies. He is the recipient of awards from the New York Newspaper Guild and the Overseas Press Club of America; he has also received the Madelein Dane Ross Award, the World Press General Picture Award, and the Nikon World Understanding Award. His work appears regularly in the world's leading news magazines.

Sarah Leen   Beirut 1983

Sarah Leen

American/Philadelphia, Pennsylvania
Leen started her career at the *Topeka Capital-Journal* and the *Philadelphia Inquirer*. Now a freelancer, she works primarily for *National Geographic* and is associated with Matrix International. In 1986 she received honorable mention in the Robert F. Kennedy Journalism Awards for her work on Alzheimer's disease. Italy is her sixth *Day in the Life* book.

Andy Levin

American/New York, New York
An eight-time *Day in the Life* participant, Levin has covered a wide variety of medical subjects for news and feature magazines, including stories on a gay AIDS doctor and a nun who operates a clinic for the poor in rural Mississippi. In 1985 he received top honors in the National Press Photographers Association Pictures of the Year competition for his essay on a Nebraska farm family. In 1986 his essay on the Statue of Liberty won similar honors.

Barry Lewis

British/London
Lewis holds a Master's degree from the Royal College of Art and is a founding member of the Network agency. He works for *Life*, *GEO*, the London *Sunday Times*, and the *Observer*, and has photos on display in several U.S. and British museums.

John Loengard   New Mexico 1966

John Loengard

American/New York, New York
Loengard was on the staff of *Life* magazine from 1961 to 1972, during which time *American Photographer* hailed him as *"Life's* most influential photographer." He was the first picture editor for *People* magazine, and later served as picture editor for *Life* after its rebirth as a monthly in 1978. His book *Pictures Under Discussion*, published by Amphoto/Watson-Guptill in 1987, won the Ansel Adams Award for Book Photography from the American Society of Magazine Photographers. Loengard teaches at the International Center of Photography in New York City.

Gerd Ludwig

German/New York, New York
A founding member of the Visum photo agency in Hamburg, Ludwig is a regular contributor to *GEO*, *Life*, *Stern*, *Fortune*, and *Zeit Magazin*. He is an honorary member of the Deutsche Gesellschaft für Fotografie.

Mary Ellen Mark

American/New York, New York
Winner of numerous grants and awards, including the George W. Polk, Robert F. Kennedy, and Philippe Halsman awards for photojournalism, Mark has exhibited her work throughout the world. Herself the subject of several magazine profiles, she currently contributes to *Life*, the London *Sunday Times*, *Stern*, *Vanity Fair*, and the *New York Times*.

John Marmaras

Australian/Sydney
Marmaras spent eight years in London and thirteen years in New York before returning to his native Australia. He has worked on assignment for *Time*, *Newsweek*, the London *Sunday Times*, the *London Daily Telegraph*, *Esquire*, and *Sports Illustrated*. Italy is his third *Day in the Life* project.

Richard Marshall

American/Saint Paul, Minnesota
A three-time regional National Press Photographers Association Photographer of the Year, Marshall began his career as a radio announcer but found photo assignments for the *Ithaca* (New York) *Journal* and *Detroit News* more to his liking. Currently he works for the *St. Paul Pioneer Press Dispatch*. In 1985 he was Gannett Group Photographer of the Year for his work in black and white.

Stephanie Maze   Mexico City 1984

Stephanie Maze

American/Washington, D.C.
Maze was a staff photographer for the *San Francisco Chronicle* from 1973 to 1979. Since then she has been a freelance photographer for *National Geographic*, working in numerous Spanish-speaking countries. She has covered three Olympic Games and won a first-place award from the White House Press Photographers Association in 1985.

Steve McCurry

American/New York, New York
For the past eight years, McCurry has worked for the National Geographic Society, pursuing stories along the Afghan border and in Baghdad, Beirut, and the Sahel. His pictures of a train trip across the Indian subcontinent were published in *The Imperial Way*, with text by Paul Theroux. His awards include Magazine Photographer of the Year in 1984, the Overseas Press Club Robert Capa Gold Medal Citation in 1980, and an unprecedented four first places in the World Press Photo Foundation awards in 1985.

Joe McNally   Cincinnati 1988

Joe McNally

American/New York, New York
McNally has been a magazine freelancer since 1981, publishing pictures primarily in *Life*, *National Geographic*, and *Sports Illustrated*. He is affiliated with the Sygma photo agency and won first prize in magazine illustration in the 1988 University of Missouri Picture of the Year awards.

Dilip Mehta

Canadian/Toronto
An original member of Contact Press Images, Mehta began his career in 1971 as a graphic designer before turning to photography and documentary filmmaking. A regular contributor to *Time*, *Fortune*, *GEO*, *Paris Match*, and the London *Sunday Times*, he frequently returns to his native India to cover news events. His images of the chemical disaster in Bhopal and the aftermath of the assassination of Indira Gandhi earned him two World Press Photo Foundation awards in 1985.

Marcello Mencarini

Italian/Rome
A staff photographer for *TV Radiocorriere*, Mencarini has worked both as a photojournalist, covering news and politics, and as a freelance portrait photographer specializing in artists, classical musicians, and writers. He is a frequent contributor to *L'Espresso*.

Jim Mendenhall   California 1988

Jim Mendenhall

American/Los Angeles, California
Mendenhall's work has appeared in more than 70 magazines around the world, including *Life*, *National Geographic*, *Sports Illustrated*, *Newsweek*, *Forbes*, and *GQ*. He is currently a *Los Angeles Times* staff photographer.

Doug Menuez

American/Sausalito, California
Formerly with *USA Today*, Menuez now works on assignment around the world for *Time*, *Newsweek*, *U.S. News & World Report*, *Fortune*, and other news magazines. In 1987 he established Reportage, a full-service corporate photojournalism agency specializing in the design and production of annual reports, brochures, and photo essays. In 1989 Menuez co-directed *15 Seconds: The Great California Earthquake of 1989*, a book project that sold 50,000 copies and raised more than $500,000 for earthquake relief.

Claus C. Meyer

German/Rio de Janeiro
The winner of many prizes and awards, Meyer was selected in 1985 by *Communications World* as one of the top annual-report photographers in the world. His color photography has been recognized by Kodak and Nikon, and in 1981 he won a Nikon International Grand Prize. He has published several books on Brazil.

Robin Moyer

American/Hong Kong
A staff photographer for *Time*, Moyer began his career in Vietnam in 1970 He has won many awards for his photography of Asia and the Middle East, including Photo of the Year in the World Press Photo Foundation competition and the Robert Capa Gold Medal Citation from the Overseas Press Club of America for his coverage of the war in Lebanon. His work is represented in the Masters of Photography Collection of the Library of Congress in Washington, D.C.

Seny Norasingh

Laotian/Raleigh, North Carolina
Norasingh moved to the United States from Laos when he was 17. His newspaper career has included positions with the *Raleigh News and Observer*, the *Raleigh Times*, the *Gastonia Gazette*, and the *Daily Advance*, and he has twice been named North Carolina Photographer of the Year. Now a freelance magazine photographer, he produces work for *National Geographic*, *Time*, *Newsweek*, *U.S. News & World Report*, the *Washington Post*, and the Time-Life book series.

Randy Olson

American/Pittsburgh, Pennsylvania

A graduate of the University of Kansas, Olson worked for the *San Jose Mercury News*, the *Charleston* (West Virginia) *Gazette*, and the *Palm Beach Post* before joining the staff of the *Pittsburgh Press*. In addition to his newspaper work, he freelances for *National Geographic*, *Fortune*, and *Time*. While teaching photojournalism at the University of Missouri, he received a National Archives grant for work with the Pictures of the Year archives.

Graeme Outerbridge

Bermudian/Southampton

Named Outstanding Young Person of the Year in Bermuda in 1985, Outerbridge is active in both politics and photography. He has exhibited work in New York, Washington, D.C., Boston, London, and Helsinki, and contributes work to *Vogue*, *House & Garden*, and *Signature*. He has published two books, the most recent of which, *Bridges*, was published in 1989 by Abrams.

Daniele Pellegrini

Italian/Milan

The son of famed journalist Lino Pellegrini, Daniele has been a staff photographer for *Airone* since 1981; he travels eight months a year in search of great pictures. He is in the Guinness Book of World Records for having made the first trip around the world in a truck—a trip that resulted in the book *Un camion intorno al mondo* (*A Truck Around the World*), published by Mondadori in 1980. He participated in *A Day in the Life of America*.

Bill Pierce

American/New York, New York

A graduate of Princeton University and now a contract photographer for *U.S. News & World Report*, Pierce played backup guitar for Jimi Hendrix before choosing photojournalism as a career. His images of conflicts in Beirut and Belfast won him the Overseas Press Club's Oliver Rebbot Award for international photoreportage, and he won the Leica Medal of Excellence in 1989 for his contributions to the project *Homeless in America*. Italy is his fourth *Day in the Life* project.

Vittoriano Rastelli

Italian/Rome

During a 38-year career Rastelli has published work in *Life*, *Time*, *Oggi*, *Epoca*, and other leading magazines. He has won the Page One Award for Excellence in Journalism and the *Premio Campione Italia* award.

Jim Richardson

American/Denver, Colorado

Richardson is a freelance photographer whose images often appear in *Time*, *Fortune*, and *National Geographic*. His photographs of small-town life in the American Midwest have been honored at the World Understanding Contest with three Special Recognition awards.

Rick Rickman

American/Laguna Niguel, California

During the five years he worked for the *Des Moines Register*, Rickman was named Iowa Photographer of the Year three times. In 1985 he brought a Pulitzer Prize in Spot News Photography to the *Orange County Register* for coverage of the 1984 Olympics, and was chosen California Photographer of the Year.

Joe Rossi

American/Saint Paul, Minnesota

Rossi's grandparents emigrated to the United States from a small village near Genoa early this century. A native Minnesotan, Rossi has been a staff photographer for the *St. Paul Pioneer Press Dispatch* since 1983; he has won numerous state awards.

George Steinmetz   Fresno 1990

George Steinmetz

American/San Francisco, California

Before graduating from Stanford University with a degree in geophysics, Steinmetz took two-and-a-half years to hitchhike through more than 20 African countries. His work currently appears in *Time*, *Fortune*, *Life*, *GEO*, and *National Geographic*.

Patrick Tehan

American/Santa Ana, California

A staff photographer for the *Orange County Register*, Tehan won top honors in the magazine division of the National Press Photographers Association's Pictures of the Year competition. He has been a regular participant in *Day in the Life* projects.

David C. Turnley

American/Paris

Turnley is a staff photographer for the *Detroit Free Press* and is affiliated with the Black Star photo agency. He won the 1990 Pulitzer Prize and the 1989 Overseas Press Club Robert Capa Gold Medal for his images of political and social turmoil in the socialist countries; in 1988, he won Picture of the Year from the World Press Photo Foundation for a photograph of a grieving father following the Armenian earthquake. His most recent book is *Moments of Revolution*, a photographic account of the events in Eastern Europe in 1989, created jointly with his twin brother Peter.

Peter Turnley

American/Paris

Peter Turnley is a contract photographer for *Newsweek* and is also affiliated with the Black Star photo agency. His work has been recognized with World Press Photo Foundation and Overseas Press Club awards, among others. He has photographed more Soviet leaders than any other Western photographer. In 1989, he traveled to China, East Germany, Czechoslovakia, Romania, Hungary, Poland, and the Soviet Union, producing seven cover photographs for *Newsweek*. Recently he collaborated with his twin brother David on *Moments of Revolution*, a photographic study of events in Eastern Europe in 1989.

Jerry Valente

American/New York, New York

A participant in several *Day in the Life* projects, Valente also pursues corporate, editorial, and industrial assignments. When not taking pictures, he helps run a food bank in New York City.

Mauro Vallinotto

Italian/Milan

A native of Turin, Vallinotto is a former staff photographer for several of Italy's leading news magazines, including *L'Espresso*, *Panorama*, and *Famiglia Cristiana*. He is currently a staff photographer for *Venerdì*. His work appears regularly in West German, French, and U.S. publications as well.

Mark S. Wexler

American/New York, New York

Wexler travels the world as a photographer for a variety of editorial and corporate clients including *Time*, *Life*, *National Geographic*, *Smithsonian*, and *GEO*. He won three World Press Photo Foundation awards for his work on *A Day in the Life of Japan*.

Michael S. Yamashita

American/Mendham, New Jersey

A regular contributor to *National Geographic* since 1979, Yamashita has traveled extensively on assignment. His work has also appeared in *Portfolio*, *Vis à Vis*, *Travel & Leisure*, and *Signature*. Honored with a citation from the Art Directors Club of New York, he has exhibited his work at the Smithsonian Institution, at Kodak's Professional Photographer's Showcase at Epcot Center, and at the National Gallery in Japan. Italy is his third *Day in the Life* project.

Franco Zecchin

Italian/Palermo

Armed with a degree in nuclear physics and experience as an actor, Zecchin turned to photography on a trip to Africa in 1973, becoming a professional two years later. Since then he has traveled extensively, with particular emphasis on Eastern Europe. He is the editor of *Grandevù*, a monthly magazine of photography, politics, and culture. Together with Letizia Battaglia, he has documented the Sicilian Mafia for several years, a project that resulted in publication of the book *Chroniques Siciliennes* by the Centre Nationale de la Photographie in 1989. He has been affiliated with the Magnum photo agency since 1988; Italy is his second *Day in the Life* book.

Contributing Photographers

Livio Anticoli *Italian/Rome*
Logan Bentley *American/Rome*
Robert Fasulo *American/Rome*
Franco Ferraris *Italian/Milan*
Silvia Lelli *Italian/Milan*
Nico Marziali *Italian/Bracciano*
Roberto Masotti *Italian/Milan*
Gary Matoso *American/Paris*
Stefano Micozzi *Italian/Rome*
Antonello Nusca *Italian/Rome*
Fabrizio Pesce *Italian/Rome*
Giovanna Piemonti *Italian/Rome*
Enrico Sachetti *Italian/Rome*
Sandro Vermini *Italian/Genoa*

About the writer

Since attending the University of Pisa as an undergraduate, veteran writer and editor Bernard Ohanian has returned to Italy to live and work on several occasions–including stints as the RKO radio correspondent in Rome and as an editor at the Inter Press Service news agency. Stateside, his magazine feature writing has appeared in *Hippocrates*, *Parenting*, *San Francisco Focus*, *Mother Jones*, the *Columbia Journalism Review*, and the *Washington Post*. He is the editor and caption writer of *The Power to Heal*, a photographic look at health, healing, and medicine around the world published by Prentice Hall Press. When in Italy, the lifelong Californian spends his Sundays at the Stadio Olimpico, cheering on his favorite soccer team, A.S. Roma.

This book was designed and produced entirely on Apple Macintosh II computers using Mass Microsystems external hard drives with removable 45-megabyte DataCart cartridges. The images were digitized with both a Barneyscan and an Abaton 300 scanner. Output was generated using Adobe type fonts on a Linotype L-300 printer. Project software included Aldus PageMaker, Adobe Illustrator 88, Living Videotext's MORE, and Microsoft Works. Collins Publishers has a local area network utilizing Farallon Computing's PhoneNET PLUS and THINK Technology's InBox to link 30 Macintoshes. We gratefully acknowledge the companies listed above for their generous assistance.

Andy Levin

Sponsors and Contributors

Sponsors
Eastman Kodak Company
Pan American World Airways, Inc.
Nikon Corporation
Bettoja Hotels
Avis Autonoleggio S.p.A.
Credito Italiano

Major Contributors
Apple Computer S.p.A.
Banca Nazionale Del Lavoro
Bedford Hotel
British Airways
Farallon Computing, Inc.
Konos S.p.A.
The New Lab
Pallas Photo Labs, Inc.
Qantas Airways Ltd

Contributors
Abaton
Abbazia di Montecassino
Abbazia di Monte Oliveto
   Maggiore
Adobe Systems
Aero Club Como
Aldus Corporation
American Express Travel
   Management Services
American Field Service
Arma dei Carabinieri, Ufficio
   Relazioni Pubbliche
Associazione Madonnari d'Italia
Barneyscan Corporation
Bureau Facilities Centre S.r.l.
Carabinieri Gruppo Elicotteri
Cervietti Studio
CIN CIN SKI
Cinecittà
Comune di Campodimele
Concorde International Travel
   Pty Ltd
Conservatree Paper Company
Copies & Graphics of S.F.
Crent Company
Curia Provinciale ofm., Assisi
DeAngelis Studios
DMS Diffusione Immagine
Dynamac Computer Products, Inc.
Eddie Adams Workshop
Federconsorzi
Galeotti Studio
Hilton International Hotel, Tokyo
Istituto Centrale del Restauro
Iuppa McCarten, Inc.
L.T.D. Transcribing
Lundeen Associates, Inc.
Maine Photographic Workshops
Microsoft Corporation
Northwest Airlines, Inc.
Oggetti
Panalpina, Inc.
Pinnacle Type
Primal Screen
The RxMedia Group
Società Canottieri Firenze
SuperMac Technology
Symantec's Living Videotext
   Division
Unità Sociale, Sanitaria Locale 24,
   Piedmont

Friends, Advisers, and Consultants

Susannah Aaron
Brad Adams
Giuseppe Affatato
Umberto Agliastro
Alfredo Agostini
Stefano Aldrigetti
Jeff Allen
Isadora Alman
John Altberg
Diana Anderson
Eva Andersson
Perso Androus
Antonello Angeleri
Sister Maria Angelica
Silvano Angelotti
Fabrizio Annini
Samantha Antonnicola
John Apen
Vincenzo Arciola
Raffaele Arcuri
Diego Arletti
Nick Armatas
Susan Arritt
Lina Ascione
Giuseppe Assirelli
Bill Atkinson
Fabio Augugliaro
David Austin
Fabio Balenzano
Rhonda Ball
Mario Ballestra
Anna Maria Bambara
Alessandro Baratta
Giuseppe Barnao
Howard Barney
Francesco Basville
James Baxter
Jeanne Bayer
Silvano Belluni
Stefano & Lorenzo Bencistà
Toscan Bennett
Michele Bentivegna
Paul Berg
Marcello Berger
Gregg Berryman
Mario Bertolini
Angelo Bettoja
Gian Paolo & Rita Biasin
Nico Blasi
Peter Block
Gene Blumberg
Phillip Blumenthal
Piero Blundo
David Bohrman
Giovanni Bonanno
Amy Bonetti
Mirella Consuela Boncompagni
Cathy Booth
Giovanni Borgese
Rita Borgo
Katherine Boschetto
Sara Liberata Botta
Mario Bottaro
Edward & Esther Bourg
Pasquale Bove
Jessica Brackman
Paul Brainerd
Mary Brasini
John Brautigam
Ottavia De Ferrari Breggia
Kandes Bregman
Helga Breuer
Marina Brizzi
Adrienne Bronfeld
Nick Brough
David Brown

John Brown
Russell Brown
Don Alberto Brugioni
Sister Maria Bruna
Cecilia Brunazzi
Lorna Buratto
Joseph Butta
Claudia Caciolla
Alberto Cadelago
Mario Calitz
Beppe Dianora Calvi
Luciano Calzotto
Maurizio Caminada
Alessandra Canova
Livio Capozzo
Conte Neri Capponi
Niccolò Capponi
Ada Carelli
Salvatore Carlino
Anna Rosa Carnio
Silvana Caroli
Franco Carraro
Giovanni Castellana
Mario Castillioni
Melita Cataldi
Anna Cataoldi
Robert Caudill
Mario Cecalupo
Feliciano & Anita Cerise
Mike & Gina Cerre
Colby Chandler
Donald Chaps
Sarah Charf
Carlo Chellini
Laura Chiaccherini
Romano Chietti
Victor Chiles
Albert Chu
Beth Churchill-Fantz
Carl Ciavolella
Alba Cimaglia
Fabio Cimino
Danilo Cinel
Mario Circosta
Scott Clair
Margaret Clark
Tony Clementi
Bill Coblentz
Norman Colavincenzo
Katia Comando
Ferruccio Compagnucci
Enzo Coniglio
Sandra Constantini
Michael Contarino
Sue Contois
Yvonne Cook
Steve Cooper
Marino Corona
Teresa Corridori
Laura Costa
Giano Covato
Suzanne Cowan
George Craig
Antonio Creti
Alberto Croce
Remo Croci
Barbara Crossen & family
Enzo Cucchi
Vittorio D'Acunto
Andrea Dagortes
Alberto D'Albora
Maurizio Dal Zotto
Paolo & Antonio D'Amico
Sarah Dandrea
Nicole Danner
Paolo D'Anselmi
Stanley Darrow
Paula David
Enrico Deaglio

Anna DeAgostini
Robert de Alessi
June Decter
Piero Degennaro
Aldo De Giuli
Elsa Delacobis
Pia De Iuliis
Ernesto D'Elia
Michele D'Elia
Alberto Dell'Utri
Anna Della Torre
Maj. Tullio Del Sette
Alberto Demarines
Ray DeMoulin
Sergio Dermo
Giampaolo D'Errico
Ed Diba
Anna Di Blasio
Claudio DiGiuseppe
Luchino Visconti Di Massino
Cecilia di Michele
Carmela Dioguardi
Gerardo di Pirro
Massimo Di Rienzo
Roberto Di Todaro
Stefania Donati
Achille Donini
Sheila Donnelly
Adriano Doria
Gene & Gayle Driskell
Gloria Eckert
Steve Edelman
Brooks Elder
Conte Marco Emo
Contessa Caroline Emo
S. Enomoto
Ron Enriquez
Franca Entringer
Ellen Erwitt
Elliott Erwitt
Jeanette Erwitt
Tina Essegian
Fabio Fabbri
Giorgio Facchinetti
Ada Maria Falchi
Marilena Falchi
Doudou Fall
Doriana Fallo
Guglielmo & Assunta Fallo
Laura Fallo
Tibor Farkas
Luigi Fassati
Lenka Fejt
Phil Feldman
Carlo Felicioni
Franca Femeraro
Leonardo Ferragamo
Jacopo Ferri
Franco Ferro
Aldo Fiorentino
Vera Fiorenzano
Sandra Flaviani
Virginia Foderaro
The Most Rev. John Foley
Tete Foley
Paulette & Lazlo Fono
Silvia Franza
Maj. Nunzio Frasca
Renato Frezzotti
Fabrieis Fuffo
Carmela Furnari
Nino & Sara Furnari
Simonetta Gabrielli
Dada Gaggi
William Gallagher
Sister Juliana Galli
Laura Gallia
Juliano Galloni
Michele Galluzzi
Marvin & Leslie Gans

Andy Levin

Marta Garcia
Rebecca Gardener
Antonio Gavelli
Don Pierino Gelmino
Don George
Karen Gerold
Kristian Ghedina
Angelo Giannini
Joan Gilbertson
Alessandra Giliberto
Riccardo Giliberto
Bill Giordano
Linda Giorgino
Sabino Giovannoni
Ron Gogle
Tom Goldstein
Giovanni Gonnella
Gemma Gonzata
Jim Gordon
Bennozzo Gozzoli
Pino Grandinetti
Luigi Grassi
Ciccino & Giuseppina Grasso
Ubaldo Grazia
Giancarlo Greco
Jerry Grossman
Nella Guarella
Francesco Guarracino
Frau Maria Guggenberg
Tommaso Guicciardini
Paola Guiso
Francesco Gurrieri
Tim Hamilton
Meredith Hankey
Missy Hargraves
Steve Haugen
Tina Helsell
Mark Hendricks
David Henning
Andy Hertzfeld
Jacqueline Heuker of Hoek
Sam Hoffman
Simona Howe
Barbara Huffum
Rev. Thomas Hunt
The Honorable Renzo Imbeni
Vern Iuppa
Sandro Iuzzarelli
Stefan Jacher
Sharon Jackson
Janice James
Anna Jannello
Giulia Jannello
Jim Jennings
Steve Jobs
John Johns
Thor Johnson
Tom Johnson
Elvis Jones
Kathy Jones
Tony Joseph
Denise Joy
Cecil Juanerena
H. Kamijo
Patty Kammerer
Susan Kare
Troy Kashon
S. Kataoka
Susan Kelly
Bob Kennedy
Brad Kibbel
K. Kita
Kodalux Processing Services
Randy Koral
Jeff Kriendler
Pino La Mancusa
Francesco La Valle
Alberto & Giovanna La Volpe
Rev. Guido Laera

Eliane Laffont
Stuart & Laurina Lamb
Stuart Lamb, Jr.
John Lampl
Sonia Land
Bill Lane
Susan Lang
Lt. Col. Amerigo Lantieri
Vito Lanzillotta
Stuart Laurence
Billie Jeanne Lebda
Franco Lefevre
Rudi Legname
Letizia Lelio
Helen Leung
Mindy Leventhal
Teresa Levi
Martin Levin
Shim W. Lew
Jodie Lewinsohn
Harry Lindinger
Rosasco Lino
Antonio Llatas
Helene Lobel
Pierluigi Lofrinch
Alesandra Loma
Pietro Lombardi
Umberto Lombardi
Mina Lomuscio
Arsenio Lopez
Geraldine Lopez
Richard LoPinto
Bill Lord
Richard Lovrin
Andrew Lowe
Thomas Lucas
Roberto Lucchini
Tim Lundeen
Roberto Luongo
David Lyman
Matilde Macchiuso
Judi Magann
Emilio Magni
Giuseppe Mancuso
Alfred Mandel
Marina Mantegani
Bill Mapes
Letizia Maraini
Luca Marani
Otello Marchetti
Andrea Marchiori
Dino Marianetti
Mauro Mariani
Consuelo Martin
Rev. Giuseppe Pio Martin
Matthew Martin
Silvana Martinelli
Carmen Masi
Mimmo Masi
Simone Masi
Giancarlo Masini
Richard Masur
Dixie Mathews
Lucienne & Richard Matthews
Diane McAlpin & family
Drew McEachern
Barbara Medina
Domenica Medori
John Menadue
Antonio Mendozza
Pietro Menea
Stan Menscher
Mauro Mercuri
Renata Meroni
Cecilia Metelli
Santo Micallef
Monika Michel
Jill Miller
Miranda Minucci
Antonio Modestini

Phillip Moffitt
Pete Mojsej
Monica Monterosso
Lidia Moore
Shirley Moorehouse
Martha Morano
Antonio Morè
Marlene Morgan
Mario Morin
Ann Moscicki
K. Muramatsu
Ettore Nardo
Phoebe Natanson
Matthew Naythons
Luigi Negrini
Natalia Negro
Ninni Nehlia
Col. Lucio Nobili
Chuck Novak
Etza Ohan
Sho Ohkagawa
Arturo Olivieri
Kathryn Olney
Rev. Kieran O'Mahoney
Art & Elaine Ontko
Ludovico Ortona
Dan Oshima
Rev. Brian O'Sullivan
Giuliana Galeotti Ottieri
John Owen
Paolo Pagliaricci
Rusty Pallas
Leonardo Paloscea
Ugo Parizzi
Federico Patanè
Renato Patessio
Cristina Pau
Daniel Paul
Giovanni Pecunia
Rosalba Pedrina
Bill Pekala
Olindo Pelino
Luigi Pellegrini
Francisco Peña
Tyler Peppel
Gregg Perin
Roberto Perini
Gabe Perle
Raffaele Perlin
Peter Pernice
Mario Perrone
Maurizio Perrotti
Emil Jana Persic
Nino Petrilligeri
Agostino Petti
Lello Piazza
Franco Pierotti
Sister Graziella Piga
Giovanni Piperno
Nicola Pisani
Nino Pivito
Martina Pizznoto
Michele Pizzutti
Armand Plasencia
Thomas Plaskett
Giampiero Pogu
Achille Porfirio
Christine Preble
Klaus Priebe
Elio Prioreschi
Darcy Provo
Don Luigi Rancitelli
Gino & Antonella Rasa
Tonino & Nellè Rasa
Antonio Ratti
Ray Razon
Gary Reed
Francesco Refolo
Rino Reggiani

Fabrizio Reginato
Gary Reid
Ennio Rendina
Hunter Reno
Antonio Ricci
Paola Ricci
Jorge Rico
Thomas P. Rielly
Fernando Rigon
Stacey Roberts
Anna Robinson
Debbie Donnelly Robinson
Rodney Robson
Guido Robustelli
Manuel Rodriguez
Tomasso Romani
Giancarlo Ronci
Lazlo Rosciweiz
Joan & Bob Rosenberg
Larry Rosenthal
Bill Rosenzweig
Bruno Rossi
Gianni Rossi
Joseph Runde
Mark Rykoff
Nola Safro
Col. Vittorio Salino
Giovanna Salvadore
Marianne Samenko
Augusto Santarelli
Agostino Santoro
Lilla Santullo
Manuela Sarto
Pino Saviolo
Murray & Jenny Sayle
Amerigo Scafoletti
Ubaldo Scarzi & family
John Schaffer
Fred & Joanne Scherrer
Mark Schwaas
John Sculley
The Honorable Peter Secchia
Jeff Seid
Vicenzo Sentuti
Raj Seth
Narriman Casati Shahrokh
Dawn Sheggeby
K. Shioiri
Judith Shmueli
Silvia Silenzi
Sharon Silva
Mike Simmons
Toni Simonetti
Lorrie Sisca
John Sither
Sylvia Sleight
Nick Slovak
Linda Smith
Marvin & Gloria Smolan
Giovanni & Patrizia Sollima
Brian Soo Hoo
Valerie Speiss
Pete Spence
Giorgio Spiller
John Spitzler
Ruth Spitzler
Lee Sporn
Kim Springer
Randy Springer
Gianni Staffoli
Patrizia Steccato
Bob Stein
Giovanna Silvestri Steven
Juanarosa Stiles
Michael Story
Lew Stowbunenko
Marcella Senni Stratta
Joe Strear
Steve Streeter
Peter Sutch

Martin Swig
Jon Tandler
R. Tanizaki
Michael Tchao
Marco Tesei
Edmondo Testasecca
Michael Tette
Victoria Theile
Lucia Tiberi
Susan Timper
Giovanni Tinozzi
Paolo & Shobha Titolo
Leanne Tom-Diaz
Pino & Aldo Tomasello
Piero Tomassini
Sandro Tonon
Neil Topham
Giuseppe Tornatore
Silvio Torre
Franco Tosetti
Daniela Travaglini
Guglielmo Trebino
Valeriano Trubiani
Alessandrini Tullio
Giuseppe Turri
Charles William Tyrone
Giovanni Ungarelli
Massimo Valenta
Stefania Valentini
Silvio Valtorta
Vea Van Kessel
Nicole Van Steenbeer
Luca Vasselli
Cristiana Vastaroci
Laura Velletrani
Gen. Antonio Viesti
Iffolito Vincenti-Mareri
Dario Viti
Joe Viventto
Frank Viviano
Greta Vollmer
Settimio Volpetti
Joan Wall
Judy Walsh
Carolee Ware
Kate Warne
John Warnock
Marjorie Week
Irwin Weiner
Fredda Weiss
Paolo Welters
Leonora Wiener
Dave Willmann
Dave Winer
Carmen Wirth
Roberto Wirth
Louis Woo
Ann Wood
Jimmy Woods
Simon Worrin
Richard Saul Wurman
Stella Yee
Heidi Yorkshire
T. Yoshioka
Costantinos Yotis
Michael & Dorothea Yuschenkoff
Paolo Zannella
Romano Zanoni
Alberico Zeppetella
Federico Zileri
Nica Ziliotto
Fabio Zoffoli
Viviana Zuliani
Ben Zuniga
Brandon Zurlo

Special thanks to Rick Smolan
and David Cohen

Bill Greene

Thank you to the people of Italy.